Protectionism and economic revival: the British interwar economy

Protectionism and economic revival: the British interwar economy

MICHAEL KITSON

Department of Applied Economics, Cambridge

and

SOLOMOS SOLOMOU

Faculty of Economics, Cambridge

The right of the
University of Cambridge
to print and sell
all manner of books
was granted by
Henry VIII in 1534.
The University has printed
and published continuously
since 1584.

CAMBRIDGE UNIVERSITY PRESS

Cambridge
New York   Port Chester
Melbourne   Sydney

Published by the Press Syndicate of the University of Cambridge
The Pitt Building, Trumpington Street, Cambridge CB2 1RP
40 West 20th Street, New York, NY 10011, USA
10 Stamford Road, Oakleigh, Melbourne 3166, Australia

First published 1990

British Library cataloguing in publication data
Kitson, Michael
Protectionism and economic revival: the British
interwar years.
1. Great Britain. Economic growth, history
I. Title   II. Solomou, Solomos
339.5'0941

Library of Congress cataloguing in publication data
Kitson, Michael, 1959–
Protectionism and economic revival: the British interwar economy
Michael Kitson and Solmos Solomou.
p.   cm.
Includes bibliographical references.
ISBN 0-521-38267-X
1. Great Britain – Economic conditions – 1918–1945.   2. Tariff-
-Great Britain – History – 20th century.   3. Protectionism – Great
Britain – 20th century.   4. Great Britain – Economic
policy – 1918–1945.   I. Solomou, Solomos.   II. Title.
HC256.3.K58   1990
382'.73'09410904 – dc20   89-22210
                                                              CIP

ISBN 0 521 38267 X

Transferred to digital printing 2003

IP

In memory of Nicholas Kaldor,
1908–1986

Contents

Figures

Tables

Preface

In recent years the issue of protectionism has become of increasing concern amongst economists and policy makers. Unfortunately the historical analysis of trade policy has severely lagged behind developments in international trade theory. For example, the analysis of the impact of tariffs on the British economy during the interwar years is still based on studies that have relied on traditional theoretical frameworks. This study offers new insights by looking at the disaggregated and macroeconomic evidence on the impact of UK protectionism within a broader empirical perspective.

The origin of the research reported here was a research project initially directed by the late Nicholas Kaldor. Although many ideas developed in this book were inspired by working with Kaldor, the work is our own responsibility. In fact, if Kaldor were alive today, he would be the first to take issue with many of our conclusions.

In writing this book we have also received valuable help from Derek Aldcroft, Alec Cairncross, Forrest Capie, Barry Eichengreen, Peter Fearon, Charles Feinstein, James Foreman-Peck, Tim Hatton, Alfred Maizels and two anonymous publishers' referees. We are especially grateful for the advice and assistance given to us by John Rhodes and Nick Von Tunzelmann. We also express our thanks to the ESRC for funding much of this research (grants B00230075 and R000231387).

Our thanks are also due to the secretarial staff of the Department of Applied Economics and the Faculty of Economics, Cambridge; the staff of the Marshall Library and Olga Peppercorn, librarian of the Department of Applied Economics; Hazel Dunn, Peterhouse, for typing the many versions of our bibliography; Patrick McCartan, economics editor of the Press, and Annie Rix, copyeditor for the Press, for handling our book so efficiently. A special thanks to Jane Denney and Wendy Guise.

Introduction

In February 1932 Britain imposed a General Tariff of 10 per cent *ad valorem* on imports from foreign countries. This represented a *qualitative* policy shift that affected most British industries which had been exposed to severe international competition in a world economy that was increasingly protectionist since the late 1870s. This book analyses the effects of this policy change both at the macroeconomic level and at the level of the industrial structure.

Britain's economic situation after the First World War

The performance of the British economy in the 1920s was unspectacular when compared to the achievements of the world economy. Although aggregate growth indicators show an improved performance between the cycle peak to peak years 1924–9, relative to the period 1899–1924, such measures are highly deceptive when reported in isolation. In chapter 1 we argue that such growth measures need to be placed in a long-term historical perspective. Such longer-run comparisons do not show the 1920s to be a period of rapid economic growth. Moreover, the economy was burdened with high unemployment throughout 1921–9, while many other industrial countries were able to grow more rapidly at higher levels of capacity utilisation; the manufacturing sector's performance, both in terms of output and productivity growth, was significantly lower than the 1930s; exports were below the level of 1913 even at the peak of 1929, while imports were rising as a percentage of GDP and domestic absorption.

In contrast, UK economic performance was significantly improved in the 1930s. Instead of falling below the average performance of the world economy, GDP growth was over double the weighted growth rate of the world economy and much better than the performance of the other major industrial countries, including America and France. Although unemployment remained a serious problem in the 1930s it is clear that the nature of unemployment changed, weakening the links with the level of aggregate demand and economic performance (Crafts, 1987; Eichengreen and Hatton, 1988).

Of course, at this stage in the discussion we cannot assume that tariffs explain the better performance of the post-1932 era. However, there is clearly a *prima facie* case that needs to be examined in the context of other policy changes and longer-term tendencies in the economy.

The pressures for protectionism

In Britain voices were raised in favour of protection from the late 1880s onwards, most notably by Joseph Chamberlain. His main assertation was that protection could bring increased employment and would therefore be mainly to the benefit of the worker:

The manufacturer may save himself. But it is not for him that I am chiefly concerned. It is for you – the workers – I say to you the loss of employment means more than the loss of capital to any manufacturer. You cannot live on your investments in a foreign country. You live on the labour of your hands.[1]

However, protection was not introduced until the First World War, and then limited to specific categories: by the so-called McKenna duties in 1915, which were later extended under the Safeguarding of Industries Act, 1921. The major items comprised cinema films, clocks and watches, motorcars and musical instruments, to which were added cameras, optical lenses, and a large number of scientific instruments, and various chemicals deemed essential for safety in time of war.[2]

The strength of the free trade sentiment is well illustrated by the fact that the first *Acts* of the Labour Government of 1924 (which came to power on account of Stanley Baldwin's unsuccessful bid for a specific mandate to introduce general protection) were to abolish most of these duties; the Tory Government restored them in 1925.

Pressures for the extension of protection developed throughout the period and originated from varied sources. One of the most cogent arguments came from Keynes who in his evidence to the Macmillan Committee and as Chairman of the Economic Advisory Council Committee of Economists advocated import duties as one method of increasing employment. Keynes argued that the inflexibility of real wages was the main source of unemployment. Given the rigidity of money wages, he contended that a tariff was one method of raising prices relative to money wages.[3] A second element of Keynes' argument was that a tariff, by improving the current account of the balance of payments, would increase British foreign investment and thus raise the foreign demand for domestic products.[4]

It would be wrong to consider that the debate on protection was solely conducted by academic economists. Apart from discussion in Government there was growing pressure from business groups and other interested parties. The case for tariffs put forward by the National Union of Manufacturers was instrumental in the introduction of the Safeguarding of Industries Act (Capie, 1980). From 1924 onwards the Empire Industries Association (EIA) pressed for increased tariff protection and had considerable influence amongst backbench MPs. It wanted not only increased protection for domestic industry but also the extension of Empire preference. The arguments of the EIA were closely allied to those of the iron and steel industry. Iron and steel was the industry most forceful in its advocacy of protection due to its rapidly declining share of the domestic market.

The pressure for increased protection was therefore an amalgam of sectional interests and various arguments concerning the impact of a tariff on general economic conditions. Britain's deteriorating external account finally swung the balance towards protection. In 1931 the current account balance moved into deficit, partly due to the expectation of a general tariff (Capie, 1983) and partly due to the declining invisible earnings. At the same time the depression activated fiscal stabilisers that increased the budget deficit undermining confidence in sterling. Under such conditions the argument in favour of tariffs became more *expedient;* such a policy would not only generate revenue for the Government and help the budget but it would also help correct the trade balance.

The financial crisis was heightened by the suspension of the gold standard in September 1931. Many believed this reduced the need for a tariff as exchange rate adjustment would ensure balance of payments equilibrium. Others believed that the exchange rate was incapable of achieving external balance and a large depreciation would not only undermine confidence in the economy but reduce the value of Britain's external assets as well as being inflationary. It was the latter arguments which were eventually accepted by the majority of the Cabinet and led to the emergency Abnormal Importations Act in November 1931 and the Import Duties Act in February 1932. This provided a base rate on newly protected manufactured imports of 10 per cent, but which could be raised subsequently on the recommendation of the newly established Import Duties Advisory Committee. This Committee soon recommended that most rates should be raised to 20 per cent and for a more limited category of commodities (which included steel and chemicals) it should be 30 per cent. These rates were further increased as a result of subsequent recommendations in 1934 and 1935.

The international context of protectionism

To fully appreciate the nature of Britain's trade policy change in 1932 we need to place it in the context of protectionism in the world economy during the period. As can be seen from table 1 Britain was the only major country to pursue a free trade policy in the pre-1913 era. Even by 1925 the limited extent of protectionism meant that the average tariff level on manufactured goods in the UK was only 5 per cent *ad valorem*, while the average for

Table 1 *Average tariff levels of European countries 1913, 1927 and 1931 (%)*

	1913	1927	1931
Germany	16.7	20.4	40.7
France	23.6	23.0	38.0
Italy	24.8	27.8	48.3
Belgium	14.2	11.0	17.4
Switzerland	10.5	16.8	26.4
Sweden	27.6	20.0	26.8
Finland	35.0	31.8	48.2
Spain	37.0	49.0	68.5
Austria	22.8	17.5	36.0
Czechoslovakia	22.8	31.3	50.0
Hungary	22.8	30.0	45.0
Bulgaria	22.8	67.5	96.5
Poland	—	53.5	67.5
Romania	30.3	42.3	63.0
Yugoslavia	—	32.0	46.0

Source: Liepmann (1938), p. 415.

Continental Europe was 24.9 per cent (Liepmann, 1938) and for the United States 37 per cent (Bairoch, 1986).

Moreover, the early 1930s saw a sharp rise in tariff levels and quotas. This wave of rising protectionism was induced by falling product prices in 1928–9 which encouraged many European countries to raise the level of agricultural protection. Under the Smoot-Hawley tariff in 1930 the level of American tariff protection reached an unprecedented height, especially for manufactured goods with an average duty of 45 to 50 per cent. Before the end of 1931, partly as a reprisal, twenty-five countries had raised their duties on American products. The 1930s also saw a rise in quota restrictions, particularly in France and Switzerland.

Such trends suggest that the relevant question that needs to be addressed is whether Britain pursued an appropriate *second best* trade policy in 1931–2. A first best policy of free trade was simply not viable in the circumstances of the unco-ordinated world economy of the 1930s.

The theoretical analysis of the impact of protection

The use of commercial policy as an instrument for economic revival remains a controversial issue. The theoretical aspects of this area have undergone rapid change during the past decade. There now exists a large body of literature on international trade theory arguing that protectionism may have beneficial effects on real variables. It is now widely recognised that the classical argument for free trade is based on assumptions that are historically invalid. Protectionism may be a 'second best' policy to ease the adjustment problems of under-utilised economies.

However, if other trading partners engage in retaliation, the so-called 'beggar-thy-neighbour' policy response, some trading partners may suffer and indeed *all* economies may end up worse off. In order to think about the nature of the gainers and losers from protectionism in this period we need to consider the following effects:

The 'initial conditions' effect
The 'initial growth conditions' of economies may affect their response to protectionism. Thus, economies that failed to reconstruct successfully in the 1920s, burdened with slow economic growth and uncompetitiveness, may have responded differently from the more successful economies. The argument can also be extended and adapted by emphasising the initial conditions of the sectoral structure of each economy. Thus, if the sectors protected in the 1930s were facing adverse competitive conditions in the 1920s (as in the case of Britain) economic growth may have been stimulated by protecting these sectors, giving them time to adjust.

The 'beggar-thy-neighbour' effect
Any initial benefits of a change in trade policy may be negated by the impact of retaliation and the decline in world trade. What proportion of the decline in world trade can be attributed to protectionism? The development of 'trading blocs' in the 1930s complicates the analysis of this question significantly.[5] The size of an economy may also be relevant in that it may influence the magnitude of retaliation from trading partners.

Qualitative policy shifts
Britain was basically a free trade economy until the interwar period. Thus, the policy shift of 1932 can be viewed as a *qualitative* shift for most industries and its effects would be expected to be different from the policy adjustment of other economies which simply involved raising tariff levels.

The Lewis effect
Lewis (1949, pp. 59–61) suggests that the spread of protectionism may have had beneficial effects in reducing the amplitude of the downswing but negative effects during the upswing. He argues that if one country cuts its imports then trading partners whose exports have fallen must cut their imports to maintain trade balance. To achieve balance with the protection-

ist country without recourse to trade policy their overall level of imports will have to fall by some multiple of their imbalance with the protectionist country. That is, they will have to deflate. The introduction of a tariff allows trade flows to be adjusted directly, arresting the necessity of internal deflation. However, if the country maintains protection during the recovery period this may hinder the strength of recovery by preventing the expansion of trade.

The overall policy regime of the 1930s

The effect of tariff policy cannot be analysed in isolation. The 1930s saw a number of important changes due to other policies and 'natural' cyclical influences. Sterling was devalued in September 1931 which gave Britain a major competitive advantage between 1932 and 1933. The devaluation also meant that the government could pursue a 'cheap money' policy between 1932 and 1939, as it did not now have to use monetary policy to sustain the exchange rate. Many studies have also pointed to the 'natural' influences favouring recovery in the 1930s, such as the favourable terms of trade between 1929 and 1933 and diffusion of new demand patterns. Many of these issues are discussed in chapter 6 but the reader should bear them in mind when evaluating the empirical results reported throughout this book.

1 British interwar economic growth in an historical perspective

Introduction

With a few exceptions most studies treat the interwar years as a well-defined economic period that was structurally different from the pre-1914 era. However, it is also important to place the period in a long-run historical perspective, if only because the initial growth conditions will be an important determinant of the growth path that an economy follows. Structural change is not equivalent to independence from the past.

A useful approach that places the interwar period in a long-run historical perspective is Maddison's theory of epochs in capitalist development. Maddison (1982) argues that economic growth has followed a number of epochs; the period 1913–50 is one such phase. Each epoch is characterised by a number of 'system characteristics', defined by:

  (i) the Government's approach to demand management,

  (ii) the bargaining power and expectations of labour,

  (iii) the degree of freedom of trade and international factor movements, and

  (iv) the character of the international payments mechanism.

During the 1930s the British economy saw a number of major system characteristic changes. The Government reversed the high interest rate policy of 1925–31 and pursued a 'cheap money' policy between 1932 and 1939; the protection of the manufacturing sector was extended significantly in 1932 breaking away from a long tradition of free trade; the international payments system changed from a fixed exchange rate between 1925 and 1931 to a managed exchange rate after 1931; and apart from these observable policy changes some of the literature has argued that the period after 1932 witnessed a phase of real wage moderation in the labour market (Beenstock et al., 1984). In addition to the system characteristics, another important aspect for phasing historical trends is what Maddison calls 'the underlying dynamics of different phases', including such factors as the incentive to invest and technical dynamism. A change in system characteristics and/or underlying dynamics can give rise to a new epoch of growth.[1]

Maddison's approach provides a context for our analysis of the British interwar economy. Our concern is similar in that we are addressing the question: to what extent was there sufficient change in system characteristics or underlying dynamics to account for the observed changes in economic performance? Thus, the role of protectionism in the recovery of the 1930s needs to be discussed within a context that allows for the influence of many other factors.

The aim of this chapter is to review the trends of the interwar years in a long-run historical perspective. For the purpose of clarity we shall present the trends for the major economic variables.

Gross domestic product (GDP)

During 1856–1913 GDP grew at approximately 2 per cent per annum. A similar rate of economic growth was observed in the interwar phase of 1924–37. The existing historical growth literature has emphasised this as an aspect of long-run continuity. This view is highly misleading. The growth path of any variable is only meaningful in terms of the initial conditions influencing the variable.

Given the poor quality of macroeconomic data before 1913 it is difficult to establish the initial conditions for GDP growth. Many of the conclusions about British economic growth during this period have been derived using the compromise estimate of GDP[2] (Matthews et al., 1982). The peak to peak cycle calculations for the compromise estimate are presented in table 1.1 and figure 1.1. The largest long-run variation of this series is observed over the interperiod comparison of 1856–99 and 1899–1913. The interperiod growth variations within the era 1856–99 are small and statistically insignificant (Solomou, 1987). Such evidence has given rise to a large literature on the Edwardian climacteric; by a climacteric the historical growth literature means a period in which growth peaked, after which the trend was towards long-run deceleration. Using the compromise estimate to capture the actual growth path of the economy can only be justified if the three measures of real GDP (income, expenditure and output) are believed to be of equal reliability. Such a condition was not satisfied during the pre-1913 era.[3] Moreover, further problems arise from the fact that biases in the data are not random. Thus, the income estimate of GDP was consistently below the expenditure estimate throughout 1874–1914, and the trends of the two series differ over different 'trend periods',[4] not simply on an annual basis (Greasley, 1986; Solomou, 1987).

Solomou and Weale (1988) question the validity of the compromise estimates of GDP and propose using a 'balanced accounts' technique,

Table 1.1 *Peak to peak growth measures and related calculations: The compromise estimate of GDP 1856–1913 (% growth per annum)*

	$\bar{g}_{Yt}(\%)$	$\hat{\sigma}_{gYt}(\%)$	$\hat{\sigma}_{gYt}/\bar{g}_{Yt}$	$\Delta\bar{g}_{Yt}(\%)$
1856–65	1.86	1.00	0.54	—
1865–73	2.27	2.43	1.07	+0.41
1873–82	1.88	1.59	0.85	−0.39
1882–9	2.20	2.27	1.03	+0.32
1889–99	2.19	2.75	1.26	−0.01
1899–1907	1.18	1.70	1.44	−1.01
1907–13	1.55	2.90	1.87	+0.37
Long periods				
1856–73	2.05	1.77	0.86	—
1873–99	2.09	2.19	1.05	+0.04
1899–1913	1.34	2.20	1.64	−0.75

Notes:
$\bar{g}_Y$ = mean geometric growth rate of GDP
$\hat{\sigma}_{gY}$ = standard deviation of the geometric mean
Δ = first difference operator
Source: Feinstein (1972), table 6, T18–T19.

utilising the reliability values of all the components of GDP to construct the aggregate trends.[5] This technique was originally proposed by Stone, Champernowne and Meade (1942) but has only recently been applied to estimating large systems of national accounts. Using information on (i) the reliability values ascribed to different series,[6] and (ii) the percentage of a series that can be accounted for by deflation, as against quantity measures, Solomou and Weale produce balanced GDP accounts for the period 1870–1913. The aggregate trends suggest the existence of long swings[7] rather than an Edwardian climacteric. The phases of growth found are:

    1874–89 – low growth
    1889–99 – high growth
    1899–1913 – low growth

The Edwardian growth phase was comparable to the slow growth period of 1874–89 (see table 1.2). A similar result is given by Crafts *et al.* (1989); using a Kalman filter to estimate the long-run trend before 1914 they find that the fall in the trend rate of growth of GDP was slight.

Thus, we conclude that the available evidence shows that the proximate peace time period to the interwar years, the *Belle-epoch*, can best be described as an aggregate downswing phase of economic growth, not

Table 1.2 *Peak to peak growth measures and related calculations: balanced GDP (% growth per annum)*

(t)	$\bar{g}_{Yt}(\%)$	$\hat{\sigma}_{gYt}(\%)$	$\hat{\sigma}_{gYt}/\bar{g}_{Yt}$	$\Delta\bar{g}_{Yt}(\%)$
1874–83	1.52	2.34	1.54	—
1883–9	1.40	1.94	1.39	−0.12
1889–99	1.74	2.58	1.49	+0.34
1899–1907	1.27	1.38	1.09	−0.47
1907–13	1.67	1.38	0.82	+0.40

Source: Solomou and Weale (1988), table 6.

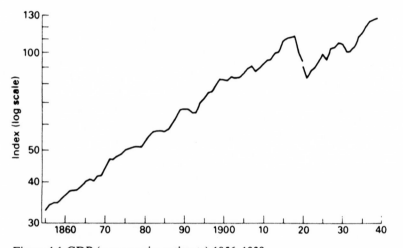

Figure 1.1 GDP (compromise estimate) 1856–1939
Source: Feinstein (1972), table 6, T18–T19.

a climacteric.[8] This is an important finding since it stresses an element of continuity in the economic growth patterns of the pre-1913 era.

The phasing of interwar GDP growth poses many problems, particularly for the period 1913–29. The statistics for 1914–21 are less satisfactory than for other periods (Matthews *et al.*, 1982). Moreover, the variance of growth is large, with GDP receiving the largest setback since the Industrial Revolution during the short period 1918–21. The cycle peak to peak dates usually chosen in the analysis of interwar patterns of economic growth are the years 1924, 1929, and 1937. Although these dates are broadly comparable in some aspects of economic activity, such as unemployment levels (Dowie, 1968), they are not strictly comparable to the pre-1913 peaks.

Table 1.3 *Peak to peak growth measures for the various GDP estimates: the interwar period (% growth per annum)*

(1)	(2)	(3)	(4)	(5)
GDP series	1913–29	1925–29	1929–37	(4)–(3)
Income	0.7	2.4	1.9	−0.5
Expenditure	0.5	1.5	1.7	+0.2
Output	0.9	2.1	2.2	+0.1
Compromise	0.7	2.0	2.0	0.0

Source: Feinstein (1972), table 6, T18–20.

In particular, 1924 is far too close to the 1921 depression to be regarded as a peak year in economic activity. Moreover, the level of GDP in 1924 was still lower than 1913, making a comparison of growth between the 1924 and 1929 and the pre-1913 cycles extremely difficult. As a way of coping with some of these problems of comparison we shall work with the benchmark years of 1913, 1929 and 1937, all peak years in economic activity; to gain further insight into the growth path of the 1920s we shall also consider the traditional cycle phasing of 1924–9 and 1929–37, but 1924 will be replaced with 1925 as the specific peak year in the production series.

The peak to peak growth rate calculations for the various GDP series are presented in table 1.3. Although the growth rate of the economy increased during 1925–9 relative to 1913–25 the period was too short for the long-run growth trends to be affected. Thus, during 1913–29 as a whole economic growth was still extremely low. During 1929–37 long-run economic growth showed signs of moving on to a higher path, making up for some of the relative growth stagnation of 1899–1929.

The long-run perspective we have been discussing is essential in order to realise the importance of the relative trend improvement in the 1930s. As already noted, the economy moved in a downswing phase during 1899–1913. During 1913–29 this growth path retarded further to 0.7 per cent per annum, despite the increase of growth observed during 1925–9. This is consistent with the view that the growth of 1925–9 was cyclical growth, where the economy was recovering from the severity of the 1920–1 depression and previous slow growth. Thus, in terms of the initial conditions, the economy had a high potential for growth during the 1920s, but this potential was only beginning to be realised during 1929–37. Figure 1.2 provides a stylised view of the above arguments. Although the growth paths between points *c-d-e* are similar, there is a major difference in that the path between *d* and *e* sees an improvement in trend relative to the long-run

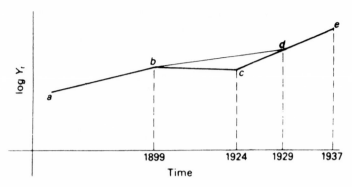

Figure 1.2 A stylised view of interwar economic growth

path *bd*; thus, the improvement of growth in the 1930s was purely a *relative* trend improvement.[9] Conversely growth between 1925 and 1929 had a very large cyclical component.

The failure of the British economy to take up the potential for growth in the 1920s is also illustrated in the poor performance of Britain relative to other economies. Britain's GDP growth of 0.7 per cent per annum during 1913–29 was approximately one third the world average and the unemployment problem was far worse than in France and America (Eichengreen and Hatton, 1988). During 1929–37 Britain's growth rate of 2 per cent per annum was over twice the world average (see table 1.4). Thus, the emphasis in the literature on the similarity of growth in the 1920s and 1930s is misleading, neglecting the differing initial conditions between the 1920s and 1930s. The numerical similarity of growth rates between 1925–9 and 1929–37 should, in fact, be taken as evidence of the qualitative *differences* between the two cycles.

Industrial production

Relative trend improvement in economic growth during the 1930s can be observed more clearly in the path of industrial production. The peak to peak growth rates for Lewis' (1978) industrial production series (manufacturing and mining) are presented in table 1.5. With the exception of the short period between 1866 and 1873 the manufacturing and mining index grew between approximately 2 per cent and 2.5 per cent per annum throughout 1857–1913. The Edwardian period saw the lowest growth rate of the era, with a rate below 2 per cent per annum.

Since we are mainly concerned with determining the initial conditions to interwar growth we shall work mainly with Lomax's (1959) indices for industrial production which cover the years since 1900. The peak to peak

Table 1.4 *The long-term growth performance of the world economy 1872–1937 (% growth per annum)*

	1872–1913	1913–29	1929–37	1913–37
Australia	3.34	1.30	1.93	1.51
Austria	2.27	0.31	1.82	0.40
Belgium	2.03	1.42	0.25	1.03
Canada	3.75	2.42	0.37	1.49
Denmark	2.68	2.66	2.18	2.50
France	1.60	1.44	0.51	0.79
Germany	2.85	1.20	3.00	1.78
Italy	1.51	1.66	1.42	1.58
Japan	2.45	3.64	2.37	3.21
Norway	2.11	2.88	3.08	2.95
Sweden	2.71	2.80	2.20	2.60
UK	1.80	0.70	1.96	1.12
USA	4.03	3.10	0.16	1.98
World*	2.69	2.19	0.85	1.74

Notes:
*The weighted sum of Maddison's sixteen capitalist countries.
Source: Maddison (1982) and Solomou (1987), table 8.1.

Table 1.5 *Peak to peak growth measures and related calculations: Lewis' manufacturing and mining index (% growth per annum)*

	$\bar{g}_{Yt}(\%)$	$\hat{\sigma}_{gYt}(\%)$	$\hat{\sigma}_{gYt}/\bar{g}_{Yt}$	$\Delta\bar{g}_{Yt}(\%)$
1857–60	2.27	6.03	2.66	—
1860–6	2.30	3·29	1.43	+0.03
1866–73	3.21	3.65	1.14	+0.91
1873–83	2.21	4.42	2.00	−1.00
1883–9	1.85	5.37	2.90	−0.36
1889–99	2.25	3.79	1.68	+0.40
1899–1907	1.88	2.94	1.56	−0.37
1907–13	2.00	5.12	2.56	+0.12
Long periods				
1853–73	2.67	3.59	1.34	—
1873–99	2.14	4.24	1.98	−0.53
1899–1913	1.93	3.84	1.99	−0.05

Source: Feinstein (1972), table 51, T111–T113.

Table 1.6 *Peak to peak growth measures and related calculations: Lomax's industrial production (% growth per annum)*

	$\bar{g}_{Yt}$	$\hat{\sigma}_{gYt}$	$\hat{\sigma}_{gYt}/\bar{g}_{Yt}$	$\Delta\bar{g}_{Yt}$
1900–7	1.42	1.87	1.32	—
1907–13	1.73	4.17	2.41	+0.31
1913–25	1.15	10.07	8.76	+0.58
1925–9	2.71	8.84	3.26	+1.56
1929–37	3.28	6.23	1.90	+0.57
Long periods				
1900–13	1.56			—
1913–29	1.54	9.51	6.17	−0.02
1900–29	1.55	7.23	4.67	—
1900–37	1.92	6.98	3.64	+0.37

Source: Lomax (1959), table 1.

growth rates for Lomax's total industrial production index are presented in table 1.6 and figure 1.3. Given the severity of the 1920–1 depression and the observed slow growth between 1900 and 1913, we would expect the potential growth conditions to be favourable in the 1920s. Despite this there is no sign of an improvement in trend growth until the 1930s (see the long period growth comparisons in table 1.6). During 1900–29 annual growth averaged 1.5 per cent while in the 1929–37 period this more than doubled to 3.3 per cent. The more rapid growth that is observed during 1925–9 is cyclical growth, reflecting the high amplitude of the 1920–1 depression and previous slow growth.

The usual argument that attempts to negate the importance of relative trend improvement in the 1930s is developed along the lines that economic growth between 1920 and 1929 or 1924 and 1929 and 1929 and 1937 was comparable (Dowie, 1968). With regard to total industrial production, the hypothesis that the mean growth path was comparable for these periods fails to be rejected. However, this focus on within-period comparisons assumes that the initial growth conditions were on a steady state path. This is quite clearly an error for the period before 1920 or 1924. Only in the 1930s can we speak of relative trend improvement once we allow for the initial conditions. The stepping up of growth between 1920 and 1929 is no more than we would expect to bring the economy back to the, already low, growth path of 1899–1913.

We tested for the improvement in trend growth in the 1930s by fitting an exponential trend with a dummy variable for 1929–37.[10] The cycle of 1929–37 shows an improvement in growth relative to the whole period 1899–1929. The estimated coefficient for a shift in the logarithmic growth

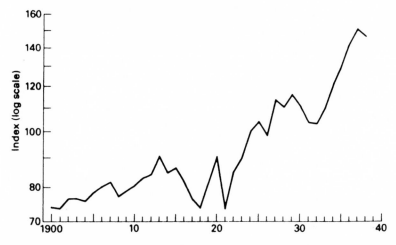

Figure 1.3 Industrial production 1900–38
Source: Lomax (1959), table 1, p. 192.

trend (δ) in the 1930s, is statistically significant (t-values in parentheses):

$$Y_t = \alpha + \beta \text{ TREND} + \gamma Z + \delta Z \text{ TREND} + U_t$$
$$U_t = AR(1)$$
$$Z = 1 \text{ for } 1929\text{–}37$$
$$Y_t = 4.2734 + 0.010704 \text{ TREND} - 0.87101 \ Z + 0.030292 \ Z \text{ TREND}$$
$$\quad\ (76.27) \quad\ (3.40) \qquad\qquad\quad -(1.91) \qquad\quad (2.12)$$
$$AR(1) = 0.61656$$
$$\qquad\quad (4.83)$$

The manufacturing sector shows an even more interesting illustration of relative improvement in trend growth during the 1930s. Once again, growth in the 1920s is best perceived as being cyclical. In fact, manufacturing growth was showing signs of retardation during 1925–9 relative to 1920–5. The long period comparisons of table 1.7 suggest that the relative trend improvement of the period 1900–37 is totally a 1930s phenomenon:

$$Y_t = \alpha + \beta \text{ TREND} + \gamma Z + \delta Z \text{ TREND} + U_t$$
$$U_t = AR(1)$$
$$Z = 1 \text{ for } 1929\text{–}37$$
$$Y_t = 4.2468 + 0.01228 \text{ TREND} - 0.91857 \ Z + 0.03842 \ Z \text{ TREND}$$
$$\quad\ (85.88) \quad\ (4.38) \qquad\qquad\quad -(2.10) \qquad\quad (2.29)$$
$$AR(1) = 0.53764$$
$$\qquad\quad (3.93)$$

Table 1.7 *Peak to peak growth measures and related calculations: Lomax's manufacturing and mining index (% growth per annum)*

	$\bar{g}_{Yt}$	$\hat{\sigma}_{gYt}$	$\hat{\sigma}_{gYt}/\bar{g}_{Yt}$	$\Delta\bar{g}_{Yt}$
1900–7	1.63	2.04	1.25	—
1907–13	2.39	4.32	1.81	+0.76
1913–25	0.93	11.30	12.15	−1.46
1925–9	2.62	5.65	2.16	+1.69
1929–37	3.56	6.23	1.75	+0.94
Long periods				
1900–13	1.98			—
1913–29	1.35	10.03	7.43	−0.63
1900–29	1.63	7.64	4.69	—
1900–37	2.05	7.34	3.58	+0.42

Source: Lomax (1959).

We also attempted to describe the variation within the two interwar cycles by fitting a second order polynomial trend function of the form,

$$Y_t = a + b \text{ TREND} + c(\text{TREND})^2 + U_t$$

to the peak to peak and through to peak phases of the two cycles. A positive coefficient on the second power of the trend shows evidence of an accelerating trend. During 1920–9 only the constant term is statistically significant suggesting that the growth that was observed was cyclical growth. This is valid for both total industrial production and manufacturing output. During 1929–37 both the first and second powers are statistically significant; moreover, the second power is positive, suggesting accelerating growth in the 1930s. During 1921–9 both the powers are significant; moreover the second power is negative, suggesting retardation of growth over the cycle. During 1932–7 only the first power is statistically significant, suggesting that the recovery was sustained on a constant path for five years.

Real wages and profitability

Real wage movements have received much attention in many recent discussions on the interwar period (Beenstock and Warburton, 1986; Dimsdale, 1984). Given the emphasis on structural shifts in the labour market in the 1930s it is important to trace the real wage path over a longer period so that we may be able to discern any possible shifts.

Table 1.8 *Peak to peak growth measures for various real wage indices* (% *growth per annum*)

	Retail real wage	Product real wage	Tradable real wage
1889–99	1.13	0.67	0.72
1899–1907	− 1.14	− 0.68	− 0.82
1907–13	− 0.18	0.16	− 0.71
1913–29	0.56	0.02	0.54
1924–29	1.10	0.77	2.23
1929–37	1.00	0.72	0.83

Source: Feinstein (1972).

A real wage index can be defined for various wage and price series. Here we use the average weekly wage series from Feinstein, deflated by retail prices to proxy consumer real wages, by the GDP deflator to proxy product real wages and an average of export and capital goods prices to proxy tradable sector product wages[11] (see table 1.8).

Retail real wages rose at a rate of 1 per cent per annum during the 1890s and fell by 1 per cent per annum during 1899–1907, moderating to − 0.2 per cent per annum during 1907–13. During the two cycles of the interwar period (1924–9 and 1929–37) consumer real wages rose by approximately 1 per cent per annum. Although there is some evidence for real wage moderation between 1933 and 1937 this is mild when compared to 1899–1907 or 1899–1913 and the level of real wages remained above that of 1933 throughout 1933–7.

Product real wages rose by 0.7 per cent per annum during the 1890s, fell by the same order of magnitude between 1899 and 1907 and rose marginally between 1907 and 1913. During the two interwar cycles 1924–9 and 1929–37 the trend growth rate was stable at 0.8 per cent per annum. Thus, in this critical variable there does not exist any real wage moderation in the 1930s relative to the 1920s; in a longer-run perspective the whole of the interwar period saw some upward trend reversal relative to the Edwardian period.

Tradable product real wages are the only ones that show any real wage moderation in the 1930s relative to the 1920s. During the 1890s cycle tradable real wages rose by 0.7 per cent per annum. They fell by 0.8 per cent per annum throughout 1899–1913. During 1924–9 they rose by 2 per cent per annum, moderating to 0.9 per cent per annum during 1929–37. Although a trend reversal is observed from 1932 to 1937, most of the decline actually occurred in 1936 and 1937.

Such evidence does not suggest that the improvement in economic growth during the 1930s can be accounted for by supply shifts in the labour market. Retail real wage growth fell between 1933 and 1937 and the trend of product real wages, reflecting possible labour demand shifts, did not change significantly. The moderation observed is limited to the tradable sector; however, export performance cannot account for the nature of rapid recovery in the 1930s.

The comparisons with earlier periods are instructive. The Edwardian period showed extensive real wage moderation and was also a period of slow economic growth. The experience of this period and the 1930s suggest that real wages are an endogenous economic variable and there does not exist a simple relationship between real wages and economic growth that can explain why the 1930s represented a period of improving trend growth.

During 1856–1913 profitability showed an irregular long swing pattern of variation (see figure 1.4). Non-farm trading profit rates were on a historically high level in 1871, following a rising trend during 1856–71. Profit rates fell, on trend, during 1871–85 and 1899–1913 and rose between 1885 and 1899, with the exception of a short-sharp interruption during 1889–92. Although this long swing pattern did not survive into the interwar period, there were large shifts in profit shares and profit rates that need to be considered when discussing the underlying dynamics of the interwar years. Moreover, given the recent emphasis on structural shifts in the labour market, looking at profitability separately will shed more light on these issues.

Table 1.9 presents the gross profit shares and profit rates for the non-farm trading sector. Both shares and rates fell significantly over the trans-war years of 1913–24. Moreover, although profit rates recovered to the pre-1913 levels by 1929, profit shares remained below the 1913 levels throughout the interwar years. The 1937 profit rates were comparable to those of 1929, suggesting that the evidence of stability in real wage behaviour is corroborated by profitability data. Thus, the higher growth of the 1930s cannot be explained by shifts in the labour market that were favourable to profitability.

Openness of the economy

Since our major concern is with the impact of protectionism, the degree of import penetration and the openness of the economy need to be documented as they are partly determined by tariff policy. Moreover, as will be discussed in chapter 2, the degree of import penetration is an important determinant of the equilibrium level of income (Kaldor, 1982).

Table 1.9 *Gross profit shares and profit rates in trading income*

	Profit share %	Profit rate %
1913	33.8	11.8
1924	24.9	8.7
1929	27.5	11.0
1937	27.0	10.6

Source: Matthews *et al.* (1982).

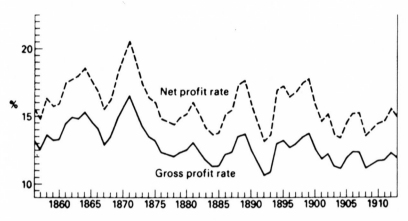

Figure 1.4 Non-farm gross and net profit rates 1855–1913
Source: Solomon (1987, p. 108).

The openness of an economy has been defined by Grassman (1980) as:

$$\frac{P_X X + P_m M}{P_n N + P_X X - P_m M}$$

where, X = export volume, with price P_X
M = import volume, with price P_m
N = volume of domestic output, with price P_n

This ratio will rise either because of changes in physical units or because of price changes. Grassman (1980) documents a rapid fall in the openness of the British economy between 1929 and 1937, relative to a much smoother decline between 1875 and 1929. The trade/income ratio moved from 49 per cent in 1875–84 to 48.6 per cent in 1905–14 and 35.4 per cent in 1925–34 (Grassman, 1980, p. 131).

Table 1.10 *Import propensity of manufactures (volume) 1924–1938*

	%
1924	9.9
1925	10.6
1926	11.5
1927	11.2
1928	11.4
1929	11.4
1930	11.4
1931	12.0
1932	8.0
1933	7.6
1934	8.1
1935	7.8
1936	7.9
1937	8.4
1938	7.9

Note: This index shows imports of manufactures expressed as a percentage of domestic demand for manufactures; gross output figures were estimated by grossing up the 1924 value from the Census of Production using the Lomax index for 1924–38. This gives a series for gross output at constant (1924) prices.
Source: Trade data, Board of Trade (various editions). Output data, Feinstein (1972), tables 9 and 51.

Beenstock and Warburton (1983) favour a definition of openness that eliminates the impact of relative price shifts:

$$\frac{X+M}{N+X-M}$$

They find that this ratio grew, on trend, between 1870 to the late 1920s but nearly all of this growth was reversed in the early 1930s with the spread of protectionism in Britain and the rest of the world.

A more interesting variable for our analysis is the degree of import penetration:

$$\frac{M}{N+M-X}$$

Table 1.10 shows the import propensity for UK manufacturing between

1924 and 1938. Between 1924 and 1931 the ratio increased, on trend, from 9.9 per cent to 12.0 per cent. In 1932 this fell by almost one third to 8.0 per cent and remained at about that level until 1938, in spite of very rapid rates of output growth between 1932 and 1937.

Conclusion

This brief outline of some of the main trends affecting the British economy in the interwar years suggests that in this study we need to explain two aspects of the economic revival of the 1930s, first, the relative trend improvement of 1929–37 and secondly, the cyclical revival of 1932–7. Of course this perspective is simply an abstraction for reasons of presentation, since the cycle and trend are not separable in any simple way. The fact that Britain imposed a General Tariff in 1932 altered some of the 'system characteristics'. At the same time there occurred an improvement in British economic growth. In this book we shall examine whether there was any causal link between these two phenomena.

2 The impact of protectionism on economic growth: theoretical issues

Introduction

Although our primary concern in this book is with the empirical evidence on the impact of British tariffs in the 1930s, historical situations cannot be analysed without explicit or implicit theoretical frameworks. Much of the economic history on the impact of tariffs in the 1930s has been written within perspectives that assume the validity of the free trade doctrine (Capie, 1978 and 1983; Richardson, 1967). In this chapter we review the theoretical literature on the impact of protection with the aim of showing that, in a wide variety of situations, protection *may* have favourable effects on real variables such as output, employment and economic growth. Since trade theory literature divides into micro and macro studies, we will use this demarcation line as the basis of our review.

Microeconomic aspects

The classical argument for free trade

The traditional argument is expressed in terms of free trade allowing countries to specialise in the production of these goods in which they have comparative advantage. Thus, by enlarging consumption possibilities free trade increases the welfare of individual countries and the world system as a whole. The imposition of tariffs disturbs the optimal allocation of resources, creates a 'dead-weight loss' on the country imposing tariffs and disrupts the equilibrium of the world system by creating distortions in the price mechanism. This classical argument for free trade is based on three major assumptions, each of which is questionable. These are:
   (i) we are dealing with a small open economy that cannot affect world relative prices,

(ii) the economy is at full employment without any adjustment problems,
(iii) production operates at constant or diminishing returns to scale and there are no other distortions in the economic system.

If any of these assumptions are not satisfied it is possible to make the following arguments in favour of protectionist policies.

The optimum tariff

A country which is large enough to affect world prices may find it advantageous to impose a general tariff. The optimum tariff can be defined as that tariff rate which allows the country imposing the tariff to reach the highest possible community indifference curve. When a tariff is imposed there are two opposing forces at work; first, there is a terms of trade effect which is beneficial to the country imposing the tariff and secondly, there is a volume of imports effect which is harmful. An optimum tariff occurs when the benefit due to the former outweighs the adverse effects of the latter. The situation is best illustrated using a two region offer curve model (see figure 2.1). Any tariff which shifts A's offer curve such that it cuts OB between N and R is superior to the free trade equilibrium shown by R, but all are inferior to the tariff that shifts A's offer curve to a position passing through Q, the optimum tariff position.

The optimum tariff represents a 'first best' argument for a tariff in that it produces an unambiguous gain in a country's welfare. For the country imposing the optimum tariff there is no internal exchange of goods that is Pareto preferred to the optimum tariff position. It should be noted, however, that the optimum tariff is beneficial for the country imposing the tariff, not for the rest of the world or the world as a whole.[1]

Adjustment costs

In assuming full employment and instantaneous adjustment to economic shocks, the free trade doctrine is grossly misleading as a policy guide. Economies are faced continuously with minor and major shocks of an international and national nature that impose the need for permanent or transitory adjustment. Such shocks may generate cyclical or structural unemployment with large social and economic costs. Moreover, many economic variables have shown hysteresis effects whereby even a temporary shock may have lasting effects. If policy makers are concerned with minimising these costs there may be a role for protection as a 'second best' policy.

Protection may help to minimise the destruction of human and physical capital by giving industries the necessary time to adjust to new conditions of comparative advantage or to the state of the international business cycle. It may be argued that protection is not the ideal policy since it is not targeted

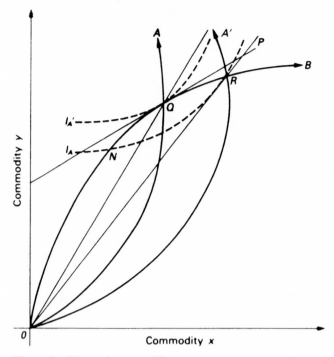

Figure 2.1 The optimum tariff
OB = offer curve for country B.
OA = offer curve for country A.
OP = equilibrium terms of trade (Px/Py).

at the problem. For example, if policy makers wish to slow down the rate of job losses then an employment subsidy will be a better targeted policy instrument. Such an argument assumes that we live in a world of certainty and we can choose the optimal policy instrument and vary it according to needs. Under conditions of uncertainty one may wish to combine a subsidy with some form of protection policy for unanticipated events.

Increasing returns
The assumptions of imperfect competition and economies of scale have only recently been introduced into international trade theory; the main reason being to explain the extensive and growing intra-industry trade between industrialised countries. The explanation for intra-industry trade flows is to be found in the existence of differentiated products produced under increasing returns. A diversity of taste amongst consumers provides an incentive for product differentiation and the presence of economies of

scale implies that each country will have to specialise in a limited number of products.

The impact of tariffs in a world of increasing returns and imperfect competition depends on the specific market structure under consideration. Such conditions imply that price is above marginal cost, giving rise to the possibility of welfare-improving state interventions. Thus, protectionism may offer a 'second best' instrument for raising welfare. For illustrative purposes we shall outline results for a domestic monopolist, monopolistic competition and oligopoly.

Pure monopoly is the simplest case to consider since traditional maximisation rules apply. The consumers are price takers and the monopolist is faced with the market demand curve. Corden (1967) outlines a model of a domestic monopolist facing imports from a competitive world industry. In these circumstances tariffs raise the price of imports on the domestic market, encouraging the monopolist to raise prices to just below the post-tariff price of imports. This increase in the degree of monopoly leads to a fall in output and employment and a rise in profits and prices in the protected industry. Since the initial market distortion was one of price being higher than marginal cost, the tariff is making the distortion worse rather than providing a 'second best' solution to welfare maximisation.

Monopolistic competition takes place in a setting of a large number of firms producing differentiated products. In equilibrium pure profits are zero. The imposition of tariffs under this market structure increases the profits of domestic firms and lowers the profits of foreign firms, causing exit abroad and entry at home. Foreign firms may attempt to avoid the impact of the tariff by setting up production in the domestic economy. Such 'tariff jumping' may increase welfare by increasing product variety and investment in the country imposing the tariff.

Cases of oligopoly are the most difficult to deal with given the diversity of possible features. Under oligopolistic conditions foreign firms are earning pure profits in the domestic market. Tariffs can be used as a tool of 'rent snatching', both through their revenue-raising effect and by switching profits away from foreign to local firms.

Although oligopoly models are dependent on the specific assumptions employed, most models suggest a role for tariffs as a policy instrument to improve welfare (Brander and Spencer, 1984; Dixit, 1984). As an example consider Krugman (1982); Krugman models a duopoly situation with economies of scale at the margin. Protection increases the share of sales of the home firm in the domestic market to the detriment of the foreign firm. This lowers the home firm's marginal costs and raises those of the foreign firm. Hence, equilibrium in the foreign market also moves in the home firm's favour. Thus with these assumptions protection leads to export promotion of intra-industry trade.[2]

In considering the case for tariffs we have looked at optimum tariffs, adjustment costs and increasing returns separately. It should be emphasised that this is purely for the purpose of presentation. The case we are putting forward would be even stronger if we were to consider adjustment costs in a world of increasing returns and the possibility of influencing the terms of trade.

Macroeconomic aspects

Since our aim is to analyse the role of the General Tariff of 1932 on the nature and extent of the British recovery of the 1930s, the focus of this section is on the macroeconomic literature dealing with protection policy under a system of flexible exchange rates. The first major contribution in this area is to be found in Mundell's (1961) seminal paper. His conclusion is that a general tariff will have adverse effects on output and employment under flexible exchange rates. Mundell recognises that, with a fixed exchange rate, and in the absence of extensive retaliation, a tariff may generate higher output and employment. However, under flexible exchange rates the adjustment of the exchange rate, resulting from the imposition of tariffs, will render commercial policy ineffective.

Mundell's result relies on the Laursen-Metzler (1950) hypothesis that saving will increase with improved terms of trade, due to an improvement in real disposable income. However, the Laursen-Metzler effect is not a clearly established empirical or theoretical result. The saving function postulated by Laursen-Metzler is an *ad hoc* Keynesian function.[3] The final effect of a terms of trade shift will depend on direct price effects, wealth effects and intertemporal substitutions; moreover these effects do not, in general, move in the same direction. Thus, it can be shown that a non-retaliatory tariff can have expansionary effects in Mundell's model as long as the restrictiveness of the Laursen-Metzler assumption is dropped from Mundell's model (Ford and Sen, 1985).

Much of the recent work on tariff policy has noted the restrictiveness of the Laursen-Metzler assumption and has attempted to see whether the result holds under more generalised assumptions. Boyer (1977) considers the impact of tariffs within a portfolio balance framework, neglecting the Laursen-Metzler effect. His framework is a neo-classical full employment model with two nominal assets. He finds that, under a system of flexible exchange rates, tariffs have no influence on nominal income in the long run when the capital account goes to zero. In the short run the direction of influence on nominal income and the balance of payments depends entirely upon whether the economy is a creditor or debtor in foreign currency denominated assets. Only when a country is a creditor in such assets does commercial policy have an expansionary effect.

Chan (1978) shows that, when a money market is added to Mundell's model, a tariff is contractionary even without the Laursen-Metzler assumption. Krugman (1982) argues that Mundell's tariff ineffectiveness result holds for a number of monetary extensions to Mundell's 1961 model. Eichengreen (1981a) looks at a simple dynamic portfolio model and finds that, with rigid money wages and static expectations, tariffs may increase employment and output in the short run while Mundell's result holds in the long run. With rational expectations Mundell's result also holds in the short run.

All these extensions to Mundell's original model have come up with similar results. This is not surprising as they all share similar features; in particular they all share the belief that the quantity theory of money is a valid description of money demand. In extensions of these models Ford and Sen (1985) have shown that, in a wide number of circumstances, tariffs can have positive effects on output and employment if the money demand function is specified in Keynesian terms, allowing for interest rate effects on money demand.

The models presented above suggest that tariffs *may* have favourable effects on output and employment for particular industries and for the macroeconomy. The models discussed suggest that the impact of tariffs depends on the assumptions being employed. However, many of the assumptions are still very restrictive. For more convincing models that can be used to analyse the experience of the 1930s we feel that a number of important themes need to be considered.

The most restrictive assumption of these models is full employment. In 1932 when the General Tariff was imposed, the UK economy was in the trough of a major world depression. Even though the amplitude of the British depression was not as severe as the rest of the world the assumption that there existed excess capacity is valid. In these circumstances the expansionary aggregate demand effects of the tariff would need to be evaluated relative to the possible contractionary effects.

Secondly, all the above models neglect the specification of the investment relationship. In Mundell's model investment is not explicitly considered and hence any possible impact from tariffs to investment is ignored. Although Krugman (1982) employs an *IS-LM* framework, investment is simply an exogenous component of absorption. Eichengreen (1979) has given some consideration to the issue of an endogenous capital stock although his working models and results assume the size of the capital stock is fixed. Eichengreen's flexible capital stock model suggests that under the assumption of no international capital mobility a tariff unambiguously increases the steady state level of the capital stock. Similar results are generated for a model with capital mobility as long as the system is stable.

Finally, despite the emphasis on increasing returns in the real international trade theory literature, these simple macroeconomic models assume constant returns to scale. The imposition of a general tariff in a world of increasing returns in many sectors and a variable capital stock would lead to more favourable effects than the current literature has allowed for.

Our intention here is to indicate further plausible mechanisms by which tariffs may have had a favourable effect on economic performance. The perspective we wish to emphasise is Kaldorian incorporating the Harrod foreign trade multiplier (Harrod, 1933).[4] Kaldor (1970, 1982) sees the importance of the Harrod foreign trade multiplier within a 'stylised facts' perspective. Noting that the British trade cycle reflects fluctuations in export demand, he argues that investment is best modelled as an induced component of aggregate demand, being determined by the income changes which are, in turn, induced by the Harrod foreign trade multiplier. Given the importance of increasing returns in manufacturing industry, this relationship may help to explain virtuous circles of growth.

Kaldor argues that the Ricardian rationale for free trade is dependent on the assumption of constant returns to scale. The existence of economies of scale in manufacturing, however, means that a nation that is successfully competing in foreign trade can expect that the advantage of an expanding market will increase its competitiveness. Similarly, a nation with poor performance in international trade can expect a trend of deteriorating competitiveness and declining markets. Thus, while not explaining what may cause initial imbalances in international trade the existence of economies of scale indicates why such imbalances may generate virtuous or vicious circles of growth.

The existence of economies of scale and the process of cumulative causation led Kaldor to stress the importance of trends in foreign trade, in particular trade in manufactures, for demand management. In analysing British post-war economic policies Kaldor (1971) argues that the poor economic performance was due to insufficient demand. This was not in the sense of an excessive propensity to save relative to the opportunities to invest but an excessive propensity to import relative to the ability to export.

The importance of the idea of export-led growth gave rise to a policy debate on the best means for securing full employment. While exchange rate adjustment seemed the most applicable method, its efficiency was called into question, particularly after the limited impact of the 1967 devaluation. It was argued that a nominal devaluation may not have a large impact on the real exchange rate, and thus competitiveness, due to the effect of rising import prices, particularly of wage goods. Devaluation is a non-selective policy and raises the prices of all imports, not just competitive ones. Consequently any attempt to generate a substantial and long-term improvement in competitiveness through the exchange rate may require a large reduction in the nominal rate with repercussions for inflation, real income and economic stability.

This led Kaldor and others to argue that some form of protection of competitive manufactures would be a more effective policy. On the other hand, since protection acts solely on imports (whereas devaluation acts on both sides of the trade account) it has been argued that protection cannot promote export-led growth. Strictly speaking this is true; however, by encouraging import substitutes, protection can expand the domestic traded goods sector. In terms of the Harrod foreign trade multiplier the means of expansion operates through reducing the propensity to import and thus reducing the leakages from the domestic economy. As Kaldor pointed out in 1951, the objective of protection in an underemployed economy would be to reduce the propensity to import competitive goods, not reduce the volume of such imports. If the policy was successful the rise in domestic incomes should encourage more imports of complementary and subsequently competitive goods.

Thus, in this simplified Kaldorian framework the main determinants of a rapid recovery in the 1930s could have arisen from two sources; either from an exogenous increase in exports or a fall in the propensity to import. Since the world economy was constrained by a slow rate of expansion of aggregate demand, the main catalyst for recovery must have arisen from a fall in import propensities resulting from policy shifts such as tariffs and devaluation.

These statements can only be understood in the context of an overall economic perspective; they do not represent the makings of a simple and complete model of an economy. The model is obviously incomplete. The income-expenditure relationship is highly simplified, the exchange rate regime and monetary regime are not considered and the study abstracts from supply side influences. The Harrod multiplier simply indicates that a fall in import propensities can increase domestic demand and stimulate output. Some of the mechanisms by which this may come about are:

(i) *Increased competitiveness*

A tariff acts to shift relative prices, making domestic products more competitive relative to foreign products in the home market. This gives rise to a process of import substitution in domestic production and consumption.

(ii) *Income effects*

The resulting increase in domestic incomes stimulates a general increase in demand that extends beyond the protected manufacturing sector via the impact of inter-sectoral multipliers. Some of the increase in domestic incomes will be leaked abroad in terms of an increased demand for imports. Hence, given constraints on world exports, the trade balance need not improve with the imposition of tariffs.

(iii) *Increasing returns effects*

The more favourable conditions for manufactures and the wider domestic market allows the manufacturing sector to expand along a path of increasing returns. Since the process of import substitution induces a higher level of domestic investment increasing returns also arise from improved vintages of capital.

(iv) *Institutional and psychological effects*

Under conditions of uncertainty, a major policy shift aimed at guaranteeing a higher level of domestic demand for the home producers may increase investment by far more than can be explained by relative price and output shifts. Thus, tariffs may be viewed as an institution aimed at reducing uncertainty for home producers which may account for some non-linearities in the investment relationship. In this perspective devaluation and rationalisation schemes may also be seen as wider forms of protectionism.

Conclusion

This overview of the theoretical literature has shown that reliance on the free trade paradigm to evaluate the impact of tariffs is too simple. There exist sound theoretical arguments which imply the *possibility* of favourable effects as a result of the imposition of tariffs. Moreover, the evidence is that retaliation against the UK economy during the 1930s was not a serious problem. The impact of the 1932 General Tariff needs to be re-evaluated in the light of the historical evidence.

3 Quantitative studies of the impact of the 1932 General Tariff

Introduction

Most studies seeking to quantify the impact of the 1932 tariff on the British economy have concentrated on substitution effects.[1] More recently there have also been a number of macroeconomic analyses of the impact of the tariff. Here we review both types of approaches, emphasising the results of quantitative work.[2]

Studies of import substitution

The first attempt to quantify the effect of the 1932 tariff was undertaken by Leak (1937). Despite employing a descriptive approach and using data confined to 1933 and 1934 Leak's detailed documentation indicates a number of areas where the tariff may have had an impact. Leak begins his analysis by calculating the average tariff level. He uses 1930 as a base year prior to the introduction of the tariff to calculate the average rate of duty that would have been levied on the pre-protection volume of imports.[3] This method thus attempts to take into account those imports that were discouraged by the tariff. Calculations are complicated as many products were liable to specific or mixed rates of duty. Allowing for these difficulties Leak estimates that the average rate of duty was 18.5 per cent in 1933, rising to 19.4 per cent in 1934 and declining to 19.3 and 19.1 per cent in the subsequent years.

Following the introduction of the tariff there was a substantial fall in the volume of imports as shown in table 3.1. Leak analyses the fall in imports across different tariff levels to test for the impact of the tariff. The reduction, however, did not consistently vary with the magnitude of the rate of duty imposed. Viewed from a theoretical perspective, this test is obviously inadequate since it neglects price and income effects.[4] However the negative results lead Leak to undertake more interesting exercises. The first concerns

Table 3.1 *Manufactures dutiable only under the Import Duties Act 1932*

Rate of duty	Value of imports from all countries in 1930	Volume of imports relative to 1930	
%	£ mill	1933(%)	1934(%)
0	17.5	97	143
10	38.9	68	77
15	12.1	80	91
20	57.9	41	48
25	6.6	59	66
30	4.3	44	52
$33^{1/3}$	17.0	36	53
Over $33^{1/3}$	1.8	90	48
Total	156.1	58	71

Source: Leak (1937), p. 569.

documenting the effect of the tariff system on the national origin of imports. Table 3.2 shows a substantial increase in the percentage of imports of dutiable goods from 'British countries' and a large decline in the percentage of imports from foreign countries. This was assumed to be the result of the concession of free entry for imports from British countries. There was also an increase in goods specifically exempted from the *ad valorem* duty.[5]

A further interesting aspect of Leak's analysis was to consider the impact of the tariff on import prices relative to domestic prices for manufactured goods. The method he employed was to value imports at the average values of goods produced domestically in the same year and compare these values with the declared values of imports.[6] A summary of Leak's results is presented in table 3.3. The first category, sample A, relates to classes of commodities of which domestic production exceeded £1 million in 1934 (apart from those classes where computation was not possible). Within this broad category there were large differences in the behaviour of import prices relative to prices of domestic products. The aggregate result however indicates first, that import prices were lower than those for similar domestic products. Secondly, there was a fall of approximately 18 percentage points in the price of imports from 1930 to 1933; this corresponds closely to the average duty imposed.[7] This indicates that the domestic price of imports (average value plus duty) relative to the average value of domestically produced products was not substantially altered by the tariff (see final column table 3.3). This could imply that for sample A goods domestic

Table 3.2 *Manufactures dutiable under the Import Duties Act 1932, by country of origin*

	1930		1933		1934	
	£ mill	%	£ mill	%	£ mill	%
Goods exempt from duty	17.5	11.2	17	18.8	25	22.6
Other goods imported from:						
British countries	18	11.5	21.5	23.8	24.5	22.2
Foreign countries	120.5	77.3	52	57.4	61	55.2
Total	156	100	90.5	100	110.5	100

Source: Leak (1937), p.573.

Table 3.3 *Retained imports liable to duty (millions of £)*

	As declared (a)	As declared plus duty (b)	At average values of goods produced domestically (c)	a/c (%)	b/c (%)
Sample A					
1930	87.2	87.2	91.8	95.0	95.0
1933	31.4	37.1	41.0	76.6	90.5
1934	34.4	40.7	44.2	77.7	92.1
Sample B					
1930	39.6	39.6	49.0	80.8	80.8
1933	19.0	22.5	25.2	75.4	89.1
1934	21.4	25.3	28.6	74.8	88.4

Source: Leak (1937), p. 583.

manufacturers took advantage of the tariff to increase prices or that importers decreased their prices by a similar amount, or a combination of both processes.

Sample B was chosen on different criteria, being those goods for which imports in 1930 accounted for at least a third of the domestic market.[8] This sample, therefore, comprised those imports that were highly competitive in the domestic market. In 1930 the relation of average values of imports to average values of domestic products was consistently lower for sample B than sample A. Leak suggests that this may be because a price advantage was required to enter the UK market. The impact of the tariff was to make the internal price of sample B imports (inclusive of the tariff) some 10 per cent below the price of similar home produced goods compared with 20 per cent below in 1930. Thus in 1933/4, these imports were approximately 10 per cent *less* competitive in the domestic market compared with 1930. Leak suggests that this relationship prevailed because, although there may have been reductions in the pre-tariff price of imports, domestic manufacturers were able to reduce prices due to expanding production and economies of scale.[9]

As we noted above Leak does not operate within any theoretical structure to analyse the effects of the tariff. Thus, the criticisms that can be levelled against his study are many (Capie, 1983); but despite the limitations there is some suggestive evidence, particularly with respect to the national origins of imports and industrial pricing, which is consistent with the notion that the tariff made many classes of imports less competitive in the domestic market, switching demand to domestic goods and encouraging domestic production.

A contrary conclusion was reached by Richardson (1967, p. 249):

The tariff had little effect on the growth of newly protected industries between 1930 and 1935.

This conclusion is based on Richardson's evaluation of the effects of protection on output, employment and trade in the newly protected industries of 1932 relative to those protected earlier. Richardson's argument is developed in two steps. The first simply compares these variables for the newly protected industries with those of other industries during the benchmark years 1930 and 1935.[10] Richardson's results are presented in table 3.4. Given that between 1930 and 1935 the fall in imports in newly protected industries was less than the fall in imports of other industries, Richardson favours a different explanation for the healthy performance of the newly protected industries than tariffs.[11] Recovery in the newly protected sector was thus seen as simply a reflection of a general recovery.

The second step of Richardson's evidence is based on calculating import replacement ratios for the newly protected and other industries between 1930 and 1935. The import replacement ratio of any industry is defined as:

$$\text{IRR} = \frac{\text{rise in gross output} - \text{rise in exports}}{\text{fall in imports}}$$

Table 3.4 The effects of protection on industries newly protected in 1931–1932 (% change)

	Imports 1931–2	Imports 1930–5	Net output 1930–5	Employment 1930–5	Net output per head 1930–5	Import replacement ratio
Newly protected	−48	−39	+23	+3	+19	3.0
Other	−37	−44	+10	+2	+8	2.0
All manufacturing	−45	−41	+18	+3	+14	2.6

Source: Richardson (1967), table 20.

Richardson argues that if a process of import substitution is observed in the 1930s then the fall in imports should lead to a proportional expansion of production for the home market, assuming a constant level of demand. Thus, *ceteris paribus*, the ratio should tend to unity if import substitution is successful. Given that the level of demand was not constant Richardson tests for the impact of the tariff by comparing the newly protected and other industries between 1930 and 1935; if the tariff is generating a process of import substitution then the IRR is expected to be closer to unity for the newly protected industries. In fact the IRR takes the value of 3.0 for the newly protected industries and 2.0 for other industries (see table 3.4). Thus Richardson concludes that import substitution was not an important factor in the 1930s recovery.

The major weakness in Richardson's analysis is the implicit assumption that the newly protected and other industries began from similar initial conditions in 1930. There is no attempt to compare the fortunes of the newly protected and other industries over a longer period which would allow us to test the implicit assumption about initial conditions. The initial conditions in the 1920s will be irrelevant only if industries were on a steady state and balanced growth path. This we know was not the case. The newly protected industries of 1932 consisted of many of the poor performing industries of the 1920s. The relevant question that Richardson's study does not address is, to what extent did protection in 1932 reverse this decline? This is a question we take up in chapter 5.

The work of Capie (1978; 1983) has pushed the analysis of the impact of tariffs in the direction of emphasising resource flows resulting from *effective* tariff rates rather than the nominal tariff changes that Richardson analysed. Effective protection is a concept originally devised by Corden which takes into account not only the nominal tariff rate on final products but also the tariffs on inputs. The effective protection rate (EPR) for industry j can be defined as:

$$EPR_j = \frac{t_j - \sum_{i=1}^{n} a_{ij} t_i}{1 - \sum_{i=1}^{n} a_{ij}}$$

EPR_j = effective protection for industry j.

$\quad t_j$ = nominal tariff on output, *ad valorem*.

$\quad t_i$ = nominal tariff on production inputs $1, 2, \ldots, n$.

$\quad a_{ij}$ = coefficient of intermediate inputs per unit of output j.

Thus, effective protection is higher the smaller the proportion of the value added in the final output and the lower the tariff on intermediate inputs. The aim of such an exercise is to investigate the impact of the tariff structure on resource allocation.

Capie's calculations suggest that contrary to the accepted picture of the recovery there seems to be little relationship between the level of effective tariffs and the pattern of industrial recovery (see Capie, 1983, table 8.1). In particular, iron and steel had a very low effective tariff rate which should have encouraged resources to flow away from the industry – or at least, in an expanding economy, prevent the sector from expanding as rapidly as it could have. The calculations also suggest, as would be expected, that the non-tradable construction sector had a negative effective protection rate. To the extent that building was important to the recovery of the 1930s, effective protection hindered the revival.

Capie's analysis is based on the notion that protection affects the performance of the economy by causing resources to flow from industries with low rates of effective protection to industries with high rates. This reasoning, however, presupposes that there is no pool of unemployed resources and that there is a perfect market for both capital and labour. A concept which assumes full employment equilibrium will not be ideal for assessing the behaviour of an economy recovering from depression. Moreover, for the concept of effective protection to affect decision making in the way Capie imagines, we require the concept to be operational.[12] Although contemporaries had a vague idea about the concept, there is little evidence to suggest that the rates of effective protection had large effects on inter-industry resource flows. Birkett (1937, p. 598) summarises contemporary conceptions of effective tariff rates:

The benefits that might accrue from the imposition of a tariff on iron and steel were always contrasted with the harm that would be done to the products which depended upon iron and steel, but we never knew the extent to which they depended upon iron and steel, and I am delighted to see that the mutual interdependence of industries will be brought out as the result of the enquiries which Mr. Leak is making, for he has provided for information regarding the consumption of the principal materials by each of the chief producing industries.

Without a knowledge of the *magnitudes* of effective tariff rates it would be difficult to see where resources should have flowed, even in a perfectly neo-classical world. Moreover, even if the price signals of the market were enough to give an industry an idea of its effective protection rate, capital immobility will weaken the effect of the EPR on resource flows.

A further problem complicating our evaluation of the impact of tariffs on decision making is that effective tariff rates can only be calculated using the input–output tables for the economy. In the protectionist era of the 1930s such a table only exists for 1935 (Barna, 1952) and Capie's calculations are provided for that year. However, information at a point in time is inadequate for studying recovery as a dynamic process. Moreover, effective tariff rates cannot be regarded as being constant during 1931–5. Relative price changes were very large between 1931 and 1935 and the pattern of depression and recovery is expected to affect the input-output structure of the economy.

In deriving effective tariff rates Capie assumes that the imposition of a 20 per cent tariff will lead the protected industry to raise prices by 20 per cent. Foreman-Peck (1981) argues that in the conditions of the early 1930s this would be unlikely. Capie (1981, p. 140) subsequently argues that the assumption is valid as 'the mood of the period was one which provided every encouragement to the raising of prices' and 'economic theory indicates that there probably would have been an upward pressure on prices'. However the evidence presented by Leak and discussed above is not consistent with this view. Although domestic industries differed in their pricing responses following the imposition of the tariff, in those industries with high import penetration domestic product prices fell relative to import prices of similar products (Leak, 1937).

The final important limitation of Capie's study is that it gives inadequate consideration to the *change* of policy regime introduced by protectionism. In an economy where physical capital is immobile, the *change* of policy regime rather than the relative tariff levels (effective or nominal) will be far more important. The change from free trade to protectionism represents an important qualitative shift in the economic system that will have effects on the industrial structure and the macroeconomic performance of the economy. In an oligopolistic environment with inflexible physical capital, this qualitative shift would be very important in stimulating investment by increasing the size of the domestic market available to domestic producers.

Macroeconomic analyses

The common weakness with all the preceding studies is that they ignore the impact of the tariff on the overall level of demand. The demand effects of the tariff have been more directly analysed by Foreman-Peck (1981) using a simple Keynesian income-expenditure model. Foreman-Peck first attempts to calculate the reduction in imports due to the tariff between 1930 and 1935; the dates are chosen on the assumption that they limit the impact of exchange rate changes.[13] During 1930–5 there occurred a 32 per cent fall in manufactured imports. At the same time income rose by 6 per cent; given a propensity to import manufactured goods of 1.44 the income effect should have raised imports by a further 8.6 per cent. Thus, a total of a 41 per cent contraction of imports may be attributed to protection. Given this fall, which represented expenditure switched to the domestic economy due to the tariff, and Kahn's estimate for the multiplier of 1.75, this approach gives a 4.1 per cent increase in income due to the tariff.[14] This represented a considerable stimulus to the economy given that GDP increased by 9.6 per cent during the period.

The fundamental weakness of the Foreman-Peck approach is that it fails to deal *directly* with the income generating consequences of the tariff. Rather than estimate the change in the foreign trade multiplier due to a fall in import propensity, Foreman-Peck relies on the Kahn multiplier which is based on investment-saving behaviour. Secondly, this approach leads to the predicted income of the tariff being estimated from the actual change in income.

Foreman-Peck's analysis is often coupled with that of Eichengreen (1979) as they both produce the same empirical result (Capie, 1983; Broadberry, 1986). This is unfortunate as Foreman-Peck's published result is not correct and more importantly their approaches are completely different. Foreman-Peck's model is Keynesian in character emphasising the positive impact of the tariff in stimulating the level of domestic demand. Eichengreen employs a general equilibrium model which by its very character precludes any *permanent* expansion in demand due to policy. In Eichengreen's basic model a tariff will appreciate the exchange rate and lead to current account surpluses. It will increase output in the short term until the exchange rate fully appreciates, the time profile of which depends on how expectations are formulated. Output and employment will decline in the long run.

The applicability of this model is questionable. Primarily it could be argued that a market clearing general equilibrium model is not appropriate in analysing a demand constrained economy. In particular the argument that a tariff will lead to appreciation of the exchange rate depends on prevailing economic conditions. With the existence of unemployment and excess capacity the tariff will switch expenditure *and* increase domestic output. This will lead to an increase in imports as income expands; thus the main impact of the tariff will be on the level of demand not the balance of trade and the exchange rate. Only under very restrictive assumptions would we expect the exchange rate to appreciate enough to fully 'crowd-out' the beneficial effects of the tariff: full employment and market clearing rational expectations have to be assumed in addition to a freely floating exchange rate. Without entering the debate on the formulation of expectations we would assert that, in the UK during the 1930s, the exchange rate was not allowed to float. It was a managed currency with intervention through the Treasury and the newly created Exchange Equalisation Account.

The simulations of Eichengreen's (1979) model present some conclusions which seem to diverge from the expected results.[15] For instance, 'one surprising result is that the General Tariff does not appear to have reduced the size of Britain's deficit; to the contrary, the effects of the tariff are sufficient to explain the movement from surplus to persistent current account deficit which occurred in 1931' (p. 207). Eichengreen explains this paradox by arguing that the main effect of the tariff was to raise absorption relative to domestic output via an improvement in the terms of trade. The counterpart of these deficits was reduced domestic stock of foreign assets. This created an excess supply of domestic assets such that the maintenance of portfolio balance generated a rise in the domestic price level. This price effect, combined with sticky nominal wages, stimulated higher domestic output.

The essence of Eichengreen's analysis is that the tariff resulted in GDP being 2.3 per cent higher in 1938 than it would otherwise have been due to the tariff's indirect impact on the price level through a monetary balance of payments transmission mechanism, with a real wage explanation for employment change.

In contrast we would argue that the persistence of current account deficits was due to the tariff stimulating income and thus imports. While being internally consistent the model that Eichengreen adopted is not ideal in evaluating the impact of the tariff in the interwar economy. In fact when relaxing some of its more restrictive assumptions Eichengreen's model has less determinate results. For instance the basic model assumes that the domestic economy does not produce the imported good. This is not a realistic assumption as intra-industry trade was important in the interwar period. If this assumption is relaxed the Eichengreen model indicates that output and employment may rise and the exchange rate may depreciate in the long run. This is what we would expect as the initial impact of the tariff on imported manufactures was to encourage domestic production of manufactures. Eichengreen also assumes that the capital stock is fixed. Yet when this assumption is relaxed he shows that the tariff may have had a favourable investment effect. Applying dynamic increasing returns would further reinforce this conclusion as the increasing capital stock incorporates new vintages.

Conclusion

This assessment of the main empirical studies of the impact of tariffs on the British economic revival of the 1930s has indicated some of their major weaknesses. The evidence suggests that the role of tariffs needs to be re-evaluated both in terms of import substitution and macroeconomic impacts. Those approaches that have attempted to evaluate the effect of the tariff on particular industries have tended to ignore the macroeconomic effect and studies that have focused on the macroeconomics of protection have been shown to be theoretically limited. They either rely on a model that is not relevant to the prevailing economic conditions or have not fully analysed the impact of the tariff on competitiveness and trade flows.

4 A macroeconomic analysis of the impact of the 1932 General Tariff

Introduction

The use of the General Tariff in 1932 as a macroeconomic instrument for economic revival remains a controversial historical issue. Problems of interpretation are further compounded by the fact that theoretical analyses of the effects of protection in a flexible exchange rate regime have generated conflicting results. Moreover, in the specific case of the 1930s sterling was devalued in 1931, the same year as the imposition of the Abnormal Importations Act, making it difficult to discern individual policy impacts. The aim of this chapter is to test the hypotheses that discouragement of imports through tariffs was an effective way of reducing the propensity to import and that the effective demand for the products of UK industry was significantly increased as a result. Much of the chapter is taken up with explaining the large fall in the manufacturing sector's import propensity in the 1930s by considering trade policy induced changes and attempting to distinguish the effects of tariffs from those of devaluation. This task is undertaken in three steps; first, we provide a descriptive overview of changes in exchange rates and tariffs, analysing their impact on competitiveness. Secondly, we explain the large fall in the import propensity of manufacturing by estimating a model of manufacturing imports, allowing for policy changes. Finally, we examine the patterns of inter-country trade flows with the aim of further distinguishing the impact of tariffs from that of devaluation. The diverse national experiences of the interwar years allow us to classify British trading partners into four major groupings. The first is the Empire and Commonwealth countries who were given preferential treatment under the tariff legislation and followed Britain's exchange rate policy within the sterling bloc. The second is the gold bloc which was faced with a combined tariff and devaluation competitive disadvantage for most of the 1930s revival. Thirdly, there was the group of non-British countries who followed Britain in devaluing early but who were adversely affected by

British tariffs. Finally, there was a group of non-British countries who were given preferential treatment under specific trade agreements. Such differing experiences in competitiveness can be expected to result in changes in trade flows. The idea is examined in the final section.

Tariffs and improved competitiveness

As was documented in chapter 1, the 1930s saw a major change in the trends for openness (Beenstock and Warburton, 1983; Grassman, 1980) and the import propensity of the economy. Between 1924 and 1931 the manufacturing sector's import propensity rose steadily from 9.9 per cent to 12.0 per cent.[1] In 1932 this fell by more than one third to 8.0 per cent and this lower magnitude was sustained throughout 1932–8 in spite of very rapid output growth during the 1930s (see figure 4.1). Since the General Tariff on manufacturing imports was introduced in 1932 there exists a *prima facie* case that the new policy may have contributed to these trend changes.

The downward shift in import propensities was also observed at the aggregate level of the ratio of imports to GDP (Matthews *et al.*, 1982, p. 432). The other component of expenditure accounting for the lower import ratio was food, beverages and tobacco. In table 4.1 and figure 4.2 we present the trends for this sector in both volume and value terms. In current prices imports of food as a proportion of GDP fell from 14.7 per cent in 1924 to 9.2 per cent in 1937; in constant (1938) prices the fall was from 11.2 per cent in 1924 to 8.5 per cent in 1937. Taking the averages for the periods 1924–31 and 1932–8 the current price average fell by over 4 percentage points of GDP (from 13.1 per cent to 9.0 per cent); the constant price fall amounted to 1.8 percentage points of GDP over these two periods (from 11.0 per cent to 9.2 per cent). Given that this sector was not significantly affected by the General Tariff of 1932 it is clear that a large part of the aggregate import propensity shift was not directly linked to protectionism.[2]

The explanation for this trend in the ratio of food imports has to be sought in a number of distinct influences. First, the differences between the value and volume figures show that a large part of the fall in the import ratio for food is due to a relative price shift between food imports and the GDP deflator. The comparisons over the two periods of 1924–31 and 1932–8 suggest that over 2 percentage points of the fall was due to this relative price change. Secondly, there was a fall in the level of food imports[3] during 1932–7 relative to 1924–31 which implies that the competitive position of the domestic agricultural sector and domestic food manufacturers improved, perhaps as a result of devaluation and tariffs imposed on non-British countries by the Ottawa agreement. Finally, given that the rate of growth of the quantity of food imports was below the trend

Table 4.1 *Import ratio for food, drink and tobacco: current and constant prices*

	Constant (1938) prices (% of GDP)	Current prices (% of GDP)
1924	11.2	14.7
1925	10.6	13.9
1926	11.2	13.7
1927	10.8	13.2
1928	10.5	12.9
1929	10.8	12.7
1930	11.0	12.8
1931	11.5	10.8
1932	10.3	10.0
1933	9.9	9.0
1934	9.2	8.6
1935	8.9	8.5
1936	8.7	8.7
1937	8.5	9.2
1938	8.6	8.7

Sources: Imports of food, drink and tobacco from Mitchell, *Abstract of British Historical Statistics* (1988), p. 475. The GDP series is taken from Feinstein (1972).

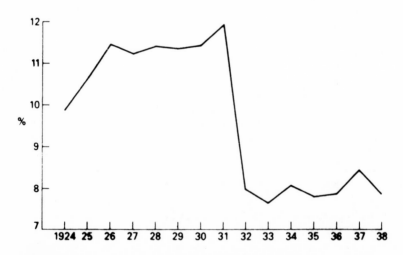

Figure 4.1 Import propensities of manufactures 1924–1938

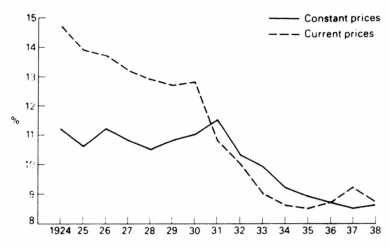

Figure 4.2 Import ratio for food, drink and tobacco: current and constant prices
Source: See table 4.1.

rate of growth of GDP throughout 1924–37 some of the fall can be explained in terms of the relatively low income elasticity of demand for food resulting in an endogenous Engel effect on the import ratio.[4]

Clearly the trends in the *aggregate* import propensity of the economy cannot be understood solely in terms of policy induced changes. However, the effect of tariffs on the import propensity of the manufacturing sector needs careful consideration. In order to evaluate this we first consider the evidence on changes in competitiveness in the 1930s.

Table 4.2 and figure 4.3 present a number of different indicators of exchange rate behaviour during the period 1924–38. The sterling-dollar rate shows considerable stability during the 1920s, reflecting Britain's return to the gold standard in 1925. This stability is also evident when account is taken of movements in other currencies; columns 3 and 4 show the movement in sterling against a basket of currencies for trade in manufactures.[5] Considering the manufacturing exchange rate (table 4.2, column 4) as the best indicator, there was an average devaluation of nearly 15 per cent for the period 1932–7 relative to 1929.

To compare the impacts of devaluation and tariffs it is necessary to consider the magnitude of the tariff. The Import Duties Act of 1932 provided a base rate on newly protected imports of 10 per cent, but which could be raised subsequently on the recommendation of the newly established Import Duties Advisory Committee. The Committee soon

Table 4.2 *Sterling exchange rates*

	(1) Sterling dollar rate	(2) Sterling effective exchange rate	(3) Sterling average exchange rate	(4) Sterling manufacturing exchange rate
1924	91.0		84.6	83.0
1925	99.5		93.5	91.4
1926	100.1		102.3	101.6
1927	100.1		100.0	100.1
1928	100.2		100.0	100.0
1929	100.0	100.0	100.0	100.0
1930	100.1		99.6	100.1
1931	93.4	100.1	93.7	94.8
1932	72.2	86.7	75.2	75.7
1933	87.3	91.3	77.0	83.8
1934	103.8	95.9	75.4	86.0
1935	100.1	95.4	74.5	85.5
1936	102.4	97.5	77.7	88.5
1937	101.8	100.8	84.7	94.3
1938	100.7	105.1	86.9	100.3

Notes:
1929 = 100 except for the sterling effective exchange rate where 1929–30 = 100.

Sources:
Column (1) Svennilson (1952), pp. 318–19.
Column (2) Redmond (1980), appendix.
Column (3) Dimsdale (1981), tables 3 and 9.
Column (4) Svennilson (1954), pp. 318–19, LCES (various editions) and Board of
    Trade (1929 and 1939). Countries covered are USA, France, Germany, Belgium,
    Netherlands, Canada, Australia and India. The German exchange rate for
    1933–8 was calculated as a 35% devaluation of the official rate (Kindleberger,
    1956, p. 116). Weights are average shares of UK manufacturing trade for 1928 and
    1935.

recommended that most rates should be raised to 20 per cent and for a more
limited category of commodities (which included steel and chemicals) it
should be 33⅓ per cent. These rates were further increased as a result of
subsequent recommendations in 1934 and 1935. Assessment of the
incidence of the tariff is dependent on the volume of manufacturing imports
charged duty at each rate. Table 4.3 (Leak, 1937, p. 569) gives such
information based on the value of imports in 1930. By using a base year

Table 4.3 *Manufactures dutiable under the Import Duties Act 1932*

	Rate of duty	Values of imports from all countries in 1930
	%	£ mill
	0	17.5
	10	38.9
	15	12.1
	20	57.9
	25	6.6
	30	4.3
	$33^{1/3}$	17.0
Over	$33^{1/3}$	1.8
Total		156.1

Source: Leak (1937), p. 569.

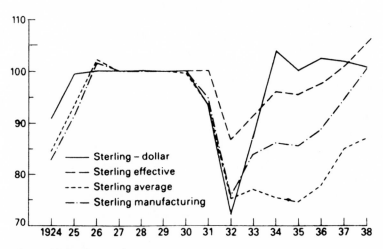

Figure 4.3 Sterling exchange rates
Source: See table 4.2.

prior to the introduction of the tariff it is possible to calculate the rate of duty that would have been levied on the pre-protection volume of imports. This method thus takes into account those imports that were discouraged by the tariff as well as those that were imported with the duty levied.

Calculations are complicated as many products were liable to specific or mixed rates of duty. Allowing for these difficulties, an average rate of duty of 13.2 per cent has been calculated for manufactured goods (see appendix 4.1) subject to the policy change of 1932.[6]

In order to evaluate changes in competitiveness it is also necessary to consider changes in domestic and world prices. A number of alternative indicators are presented in table 4.4 and figure 4.4. The real sterling index in column 1 is derived from the manufacturing index in table 4.2 adjusted for movements in relative wholesale prices. This indicator shows that following the return to the gold standard in 1925 there was an effective depreciation of the real exchange rate due to a relative decline in UK prices. It is questionable however whether this depreciation led to increased competitiveness or higher real income in sectors supplying exports and import substitutes (Dimsdale, 1981, p. 320). Following the suspension of the gold standard the real exchange rate depreciated by some 16 per cent in 1932 but by 1937 this improvement in competitiveness was eroded. The average real depreciation for manufactures was only 6 per cent for the period 1932–7 compared with the 1929 level. The relative rise in UK prices in this period served to substantially diminish its impact on competitiveness.

The use of the real exchange rate as a measure of competitiveness is limited by a number of factors (Durand and Giorno, 1987). As we are analysing trade in manufactures the use of wholesale price indices as deflators for the nominal index is not ideal because they include the prices of non-manufactures. However, adequate indices for manufactures do not exist for the countries included in our index. A second problem is that the real exchange rate does not allow for differences in pricing strategy following a change in the nominal exchange rate. To help overcome these problems we have calculated separate indices for export and import competitiveness, the latter including the impact of the tariff. The former (column 2, table 4.4) shows the unit value of UK manufacturing exports relative to the world price of manufactures, both measured in gold. This index shows a similar trend to the real exchange rate in the period 1932–7 although the average depreciation is only 2.5 per cent relative to 1929.

The import competitiveness index (column 3, table 4.4) shows the price of home sales of manufactures relative to the unit value of manufacturing imports adjusted for an average duty payable (see appendix 4.1) both measured in sterling. This index shows an average improvement in the competitiveness of domestic manufactures between 1932–7 of 5.4 per cent compared with 1929 and over 7 per cent if comparison is made with the alternative policy period of 1925–31.

Thus, the competitive advantage of a substantial nominal devaluation was significantly reduced by the induced increase in prices so that there was

Table 4.4 *Measures of competitiveness*

	(1) Real sterling manufacturing exchange rate	(2) Export competitiveness	(3) Import competitiveness
1924	106.7	98.1	103.6
1925	109.6	101.7	105.0
1926	104.3	98.7	105.9
1927	101.2	100.4	106.4
1928	100.0	98.1	102.8
1929	100.0	100.0	100.0
1930	100.7	102.7	96.6
1931	96.9	103.4	102.3
1932	83.4	91.2	93.4
1933	91.8	95.1	95.5
1934	94.6	97.9	92.9
1935	90.5	98.1	93.0
1936	96.4	100.8	96.8
1937	106.4	101.9	96.0
1938	106.0	104.6	99.9

Sources:
Column (1) Column 4, table 4.2 adjusted for differences in wholesale prices (from Mitchell, 1980, 1982 and 1983).
Column (2) Lewis (1952) and Board of Trade (various editions). Index shows unit value of manufacturing exports divided by world price of manufactures, both measured in gold.
Column (3) Feinstein (1972), BSO (1978), Board of Trade (various editions) and Leak (1937). Index shows price of home sales of manufactures divided by unit values of imports adjusted for manufacturing tariff rates reported in appendix 4.1.

only a small increase in competitiveness for UK manufacturing exports. There was, however, a larger improvement in the competitiveness of domestic manufactures relative to imports. This was primarily due to the imposition of the tariff with devaluation also making a smaller contribution.

Implicit in the preceding analysis has been the assumption that exchange depreciation and the tariff can be considered as independent policies. While this is a simplifying assumption we believe that the widely accepted idea that tariffs and devaluation counteract each other is not applicable to the UK during the 1930s. It is commonly contended that if a tariff is imposed it, through discouraging imports, will generate a trade surplus. This will

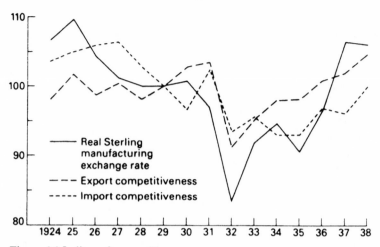

Figure 4.4 Indices of competitiveness

Source: See table 4.4.

consequently cause the exchange rate to appreciate to restore a trade balance. In the UK during the 1930s, however, the exchange rate was not allowed to float. It was a managed currency with intervention particularly through the Treasury and the newly created Exchange Equalisation Account. More importantly, even if the exchange rate had been allowed to float it would not have eliminated the tariff's expansionary impact due to the prevailing conditions of unemployment and excess capacity. The primary effect of the tariff was to increase the level of economic activity. While it may have reduced total imports in the very short term, the increase in income and output induced a rise in imports in the medium term.

An additional consideration is that the tariff may have led to a revaluation of the *real* exchange rate. Our contention is that the nominal devaluation did increase domestic costs and prices of manufactures but the impact of the tariff was less conclusive. As the devaluation did not discriminate between complementary and competitive imports it directly increased raw material costs and the prices of wage goods. The tariff however was directed at competitive goods and thus should have had a limited impact on costs.[7] It could also be argued that the imposition of a tariff would have led domestic producers of import substitutes to raise their prices by the amount of the tariff. Leak (1937) shows that domestic producers' pricing responses to tariffs were not systematic and suggests that many firms were able to decrease prices due to economies of scale (see chapter 3). Thus, for many firms, the increase in profits during the period most probably came from increased sales not higher margins.

Both devaluation and import duties were important in altering the long-term trends in trade performance which constrained UK growth in the interwar period. The devaluation of 1931 has featured prominently in the literature as a major cause of recovery in the period 1932–7. Our evidence suggests however that the resulting improvement in competitiveness was significantly eroded by the increase in domestic prices and costs. On the export side the evidence suggests that devaluation did help to halt the long-term decline in the UK share of world manufacturing exports for a relatively short period of three to four years. Britain's manufacturing exports had become seriously uncompetitive by 1930; devaluation was necessary to restore competitiveness to a more 'normal' position.

Import propensities for manufactured goods had been rising up to 1931 and we would expect devaluation to help halt such a rising trend. But in 1932 there was a *sharp fall* in the import propensity of UK manufactures of about one third (see figure 4.1), and this was sustained from 1932 through to 1938. This fall was not matched by any sustained parallel increase in the export share. There must be a strong presumption, therefore, that the large fall in import propensities was caused largely by the increased competitiveness of the domestic manufacturing industry following the extension of tariffs in 1931/2, on top of the benefits of a 'corrective' devaluation.

Manufacturing import functions

The qualitative analysis of the previous section suggests that the General Tariff of 1932 was important in explaining the fall in the manufacturing sector's import propensity in the 1930s. In this section we test this idea by estimating various import functions for UK manufacturing imports during the period 1924-38.

Making the simplifying assumptions of imperfect substitution between home and overseas goods and infinite supply elasticities at home and abroad (Houthakker and Magee, 1969), we can specify the import function for UK manufactures as:

$$M = a + b_1 Y + b_2 P + b_3 \tau + \varepsilon_t \tag{1}$$

where

M = manufacturing imports in constant prices

Y = real GDP

P = relative price of foreign to home manufactures,

   implicitly including the effect of devaluation

τ = *ad-valorem* tariff rate

Table 4.5 *OLS regression results for UK manufacturing import function 1924–1938 (t values in parenthesis)*

Results regressing:			

$\ln M = \alpha + \beta_1 \ln Y + \beta_2 \ln P + \beta_3 \tau + \varepsilon_t$

$\hat{\alpha}$	−6.772	−(1.83)	$\bar{R}^2 = 0.89$
β_1	2.114	(7.41)	DW = 2.07
β_2	−1.064	−(1.86)	F = 37.02
β_3	−0.034	(10.30)	

Notes: ln P relates to the lag of the price variable.

The tariff rate used aims to capture the effect of the policy change in 1932 and takes the value of zero between 1924 and 1931 and the manufacturing average tariff rate reported in appendix table A4.1 between 1932 and 1938.

Table 4.6 *OLS regression results for UK manufacturing import function 1924–38 (t values in parenthesis)*

Results regressing:			

$\ln M = \alpha + \beta_1 \ln Y + \beta_2 \ln P + \beta_3 \tau + \varepsilon_t$

$\hat{\alpha}$	−6.801	−(1.83)	$\bar{R}^2 = 0.89$
β_1	2.121	(7.41)	DW = 2.08
β_2	−1.071	−(1.87)	F = 36.87
β_3	−0.026	−(10.28)	

Notes: ln P relates to the lag of the relative price variable.

The tariff rate used takes the value of zero between 1924 and 1931 and Leak's series for 1932–8 (see appendix table A4.1).

By specifying the import function in this form we can explicitly consider the impact of the tariff.

Given that we expect a logarithmic relationship between income and manufacturing imports we estimate the logarithmic specification of equation (1):

$$\ln M = \alpha + \beta_1 \ln Y + \beta_2 \ln P + \beta_3 \tau + \varepsilon_t \qquad (2)$$

The only variable that is not expressed in logs is the tariff indicator which is already expressed as a percentage. The results for estimating equation (2) for a number of tariff indicators are presented in tables 4.5 and 4.6. The fit reported in both tables gives an R^2 value of 0.89. All the variables have the expected sign and the income and tariff coefficients are statistically significant at the 99 per cent confidence level. The relative price variable is statistically significant only at the 95 per cent level (one tailed test). Similar results are obtained for other tariff indicators.[8] The results suggest that UK manufacturing imports were income elastic with an elasticity above 2. The tariff had a large depressing effect on import demand; a one percentage point increase in *ad valorem* tariff rates resulted in a 2.6 to 3.4 percentage change in manufacturing imports.[9] The relative price effect is significantly smaller; a 1 per cent change in relative prices gave rise to a 1.1 per cent change in manufactured imports.

These results suggest that the impact of tariffs did not work through a simple price mechanism; the tariff effect was significantly higher than the non-tariff relative price effect.[10] One interpretation may be that the tariff was capturing a long-run price elasticity of demand for imports which was significantly higher than the short-run elasticity (Morgan and Martin, 1975).

Trade policy and the distribution of imports

Given the results so far we would expect that the changes in the distribution of trade in the 1930s were influenced more by the tariffs than by devaluation. The General Tariff did not affect imports via a simple relative price effect; the evidence presented in the last section above is consistent with the view that the General Tariff influenced the economy via feedback effects on investment and import substitution. To help us assess the reliability of these results we have examined the changing pattern of UK imports in the 1930s, by evaluating the changes in the share originating from various trading blocs.[11] Britain's trading partners have been classified into the following five blocs:

(i) the British countries, who were favoured by Imperial Preference and devalued early with Britain,[12]

(ii) the gold bloc economies[13] who were faced with tariffs and a competitive devaluation disadvantage,

(iii) the major 'core' industrial competitors (Germany and America) who were mainly affected by the General Tariff since they devalued early in the 1930s,

(iv) the non-British countries who negotiated favourable trade agreements for manufacturing products,[14]

(v) the rest of the world group, which is taken to include all countries not belonging to one of the above blocs.[15]

Such a varied sample of countries will allow us to shed more light on the

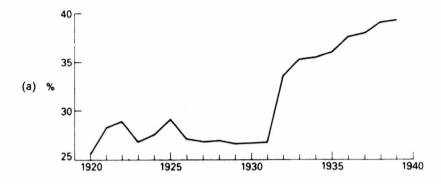

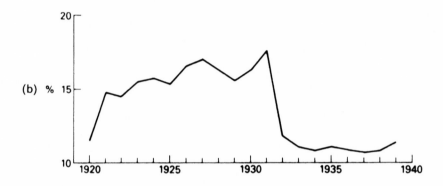

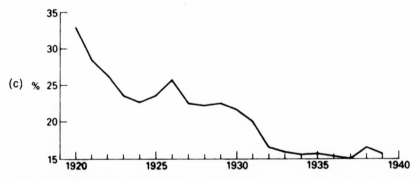

Figure 4.5 The shares of UK imports 1920–1939
(a) British countries
(b) Gold bloc
(c) Core competitors

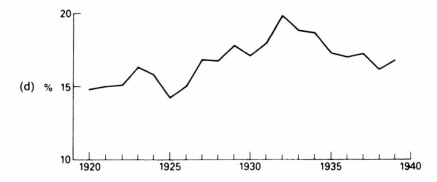

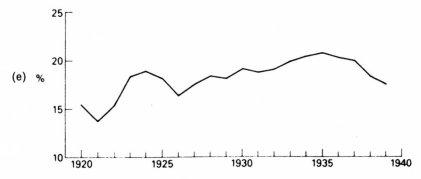

(Figure 4.5 cont.)

(d) Non-British trade agreement countries

(e) Rest of the world

Sources: Annual statement of trade of the United Kingdom, HMSO, London (1921, 1925, 1929, 1933, 1935, 1939).

effect of devaluation and tariffs on British imports. If tariffs and devaluation were both important influences on British trade we should observe a clear ranking in the changes in the shares of imports from the different blocs: at the two extremes the British countries are expected to have gained the most and the gold bloc is expected to have been most adversely affected.[16] Of course policy changes would not be the only factor determining the trends of the 1930s relative to the past; for example, given the degree of 'relative backwardness' in many of the 'British countries' and rest of the world group we would expect their path of development to influence their export performance.

A change in trade policy would also have a differential impact depending on the class of the commodity. Since devaluation is a non-discriminatory policy it is expected to affect all goods. The General Tariff was, however, more selective in its incidence, being placed on manufactured goods and non-British food imports.[17] Most imports of raw materials were free of duty. Furthermore, given the high degree of import substitution that is possible in manufacturing, we would expect that the shares of manufacturing imports would be most sensitive to trade policy changes. The diverse categories of trading blocs thus increase the number of useful comparisons significantly.

Figure 4.5 shows the share of total imports from all five 'blocs'. In order to evaluate the effects of the policy regime changes of 1931–2 we have estimated OLS regression trends for import shares for the two periods, 1924–31 and 1931–7. The inter-period differences in trends will be used to describe the observed changes after the policy reversal.[18] As can be seen from table 4.7 the trend in the share of British countries increased by 1.53 percentage points per annum between 1931 and 1937 while it fell by 0.23 percentage points per annum during 1924–31. Thus, allowing for the falling initial trend, the inter-period comparisons show that the share of imports from British countries rose by 1.76 percentage points per annum during 1931–7. The share of the gold bloc fell by 0.81 percentage points per annum. The share of the core competitors also fell in the 1931–7 period; however the underlying trend was negative throughout 1924–31 implying a deterioration of only 0.15 percentage points per annum during the inter-period comparisons of 1924–31 and 1931–7. The non-British trade agreement countries saw an inter-period trend fall of 0.78 percentage points per annum, a magnitude comparable to the gold bloc economies. The rest of the world saw an improvement in trend of 0.26 percentage points per annum.

Thus, although the relationship presented in table 4.7 does not show a perfect ranking between degree of competitiveness changes and changes in shares, there exists a reasonable fit for much of the world economy. For example, the share changes of British countries, the gold bloc and core competitors are consistent with the presence of a tariff and a devaluation effect. However, there are important anomalies that should guide us away from drawing erroneous inferences. The rest of the world group improved its share in British imports despite the adverse effect of the tariff, and the trade agreement countries showed a deterioration comparable to the gold bloc economies despite their more favourable competitive position. Such diverse behaviour implies that it is incorrect to argue that the gain of British countries was *all* due to Imperial Preference.[19] Not only was there a rising trend for the share of imports from British countries between 1870 and 1937 (Capie, 1983) but the experience of the rest of the world group shows that some of the gain in the share of British countries may have been due to

Table 4.7 Ordinary least squares trends in the shares of UK total imports, current prices (t-statistics in parenthesis)

Trading bloc	Annual % change		Inter-period trend differences
	(1)	(2)	
	Trend coefficients for 1924–31	Trend coefficients for 1931–7	
British countries	−0.23 (−2.23)*	1.53 (3.86)*	1.76
Gold bloc	0.17 (1.63)	−0.81 −(2.20)*	−0.81
Core competitors	−0.47 (−2.36)*	−0.62 −(2.96)	−0.15
Non-British trade agreement countries	0.45 (3.69)*	−0.33 −(2.15)*	−0.78
Rest of the world	0.11 (0.82)	0.26 (2.55)*	0.26

Notes:
*Significant at 95 per cent confidence level (one-tailed test).
Where the t-statistic is not significant we take the actual value of the coefficient to be equal to zero.

similar factors as those that were giving rise to an increase in the share of the rest of the world. Thus, the pattern of development of these *types* of economies could account for some of the increase. However, the differences in the magnitudes of the changes of the two groups show clearly that there was a large Imperial Preference effect in 1931–7.[20]

The behaviour of the shares of manufacturing imports (see figure 4.6) is the most important indicator of the effect of tariffs given the relatively high price elasticity of demand for manufactures and the high degree of import substitution that is possible. Table 4.8 shows that the British countries' inter-period trend grew by 2.1 percentage points per annum during 1931–7 relative to 1924–31. The gold bloc and core competitors saw trend changes of − 1.35 and − 1.67 per cent per annum respectively. The non-British trade agreement countries managed to sustain their shares, improving their position relative to the gold bloc and the core competitors. The rest of the world group gained significantly in manufactures, improving an already rising trend between 1924 and 1931 by nearly one percentage point per annum.

The pattern of manufacturing import shares observed in table 4.8 presents a fairly consistent picture for distinguishing the impact of the tariff, as against devaluation. For example, the gold bloc economies in fact were not as adversely affected as the core competitors,[21] despite their relatively over-valued currencies, and the non-British trade agreement countries saw a much better performance than the 'core competitors' despite comparable exchange rate policies.[22] The only exception in this general pattern was the rapidly increasing share of the rest of the world category. Part of this improved performance can be explained by specific factors. In particular the residual group includes Persia/Iran and the Dutch West Indies, both of which increased their exports to the UK; mainly oil from the former and cotton goods from the latter. Both these commodities were categorised as manufactures at the time while a more appropriate classification would have been as raw material inputs. However, even allowing for these specific effects the position of the rest of the world group improved relative to all other non-British groups.[23] As noted above this suggests that the stage of 'relative backwardness' needs to be considered as an important influence on their export performance. Thus, some of the increase in the British countries' share should be attributed to the *type* of economy and not to policy changes. Nevertheless the differences in the magnitudes of the trend changes between British countries and the rest of the world suggest a significant Imperial Preference effect.

The limited extent of import substitution that was possible in food production in the 1930s meant that the relative price effect, induced by tariffs and devaluation, was expected to be important in determining import

Table 4.8 Ordinary least squares trends in the shares of UK manufacturing imports, current prices (t-statistics in parenthesis)

Trading bloc	Annual % change		Inter-period trend differences
	(1)	(2)	
	Trend coefficients for 1924–31	Trend coefficients for 1931–7	
British countries	−0.61 (2.49)*	1.90 (4.89)*	2.06
Gold bloc	−0.86 −(4.75)*	−2.21 −(4.59)*	−1.35
Core competitors	0.51 (2.71)*	−1.16 −(2.88)*	−1.67
Non-British trade agreement countries	0.10 (2.89)*	0.20 −(1.74)	−0.10
Rest of the world	0.40 (2.63)*	1.27 (3.36)*	0.87

Notes:
*Significant at 95 per cent confidence level (one-tailed test).
Where the t-statistic is not significant we take the actual value of the coefficient to be equal to zero.

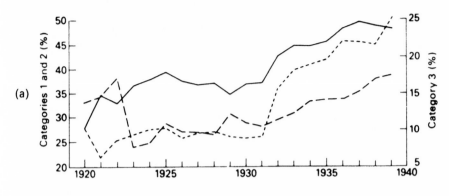

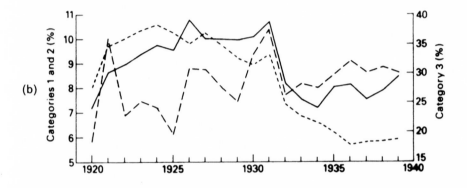

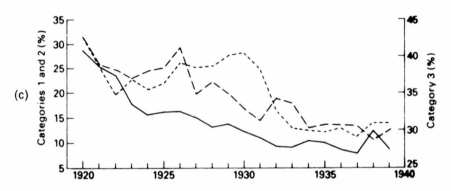

Figure 4.6 The shares of UK imports, by commodity 1920–1939

(a) British countries
(b) Gold bloc
(c) Core competitors

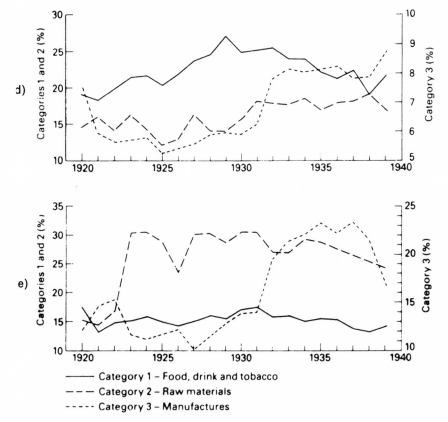

d)

e)

Category 1 – Food, drink and tobacco
– – – Category 2 – Raw materials
- - - - - Category 3 – Manufactures

Figure 4.6. *contd*—

(d) Non-British trade agreement countries

(e) Rest of the world

Sources: Annual statement of trade of the United Kingdom, HMSO, London (1921, 1925, 1929, 1933, 1935, 1939).

shares. The evidence presented in table 4.9 and figure 4.6 suggests that this was the case when we compare British countries, the gold bloc and the core competitors. The British countries gained the most, the gold bloc lost the most, and the core competitors saw a small improvement in trend. The change in the share of the non-British trade agreement countries and the rest of the world group shows that relative prices were not the only influence. Both these groups saw a deteriorating share in the 1930s suggesting that their pattern of internal growth was changing towards manufacturing.

Given that raw materials entered the UK duty free we would expect to

Table 4.9 Ordinary least squares trends in the shares of UK food imports, current prices (t-statistics in parenthesis)

| Trading bloc | Annual % change | | Inter-period trend differences |
	(1) Trend coefficients for 1924–31	(2) Trend coefficients for 1931–7	
British countries	−0.31 −(1.76)	1.74 (6.15)*	1.74
Gold bloc	0.08 (1.25)	−0.32 −(1.67)	0.0
Core competitors	−0.73 −(5.92)*	−0.32 −(2.05)*	0.41
Non-British trade agreement countries	0.75 (3.75)*	−0.67 −(4.65)*	−1.42
Rest of the world	0.31 (2.46)*	−0.45 −(4.20)*	−0.76

Notes:
*Significant at 95 per cent confidence level (one-tailed test).
Where the t-statistic is not significant we take the actual value of the coefficient to be equal to zero.

observe the impact of devaluation most clearly in this category. As expected, given the smaller competitive changes in this category, the shifts in shares were smaller than for food and manufactures. The share of British countries rose in the inter-period trend comparisons by between 1 and 2 per cent per annum, the gold bloc share fell by 0.4 per cent per annum and the core competitor's share improved by 1–63 per cent per annum, suggesting that they gained from the gold bloc overvaluation (see table 4.10). These patterns are consistent with a devaluation effect. The deterioration in the performance of the non-British trade agreement group, even relative to the gold bloc, may have been due to the increasing internal demands for raw material shares because of the demands of domestic import substitution.[25]

The evidence presented in this section is best interpreted in conjunction with the previous results. A study of manufacturing import shares does suggest that the impact of the General Tariff was more discernible than the effects of devaluation. Thus, this is further evidence that the fall in import propensities induced by tariffs was part of a complicated import substitution process rather than being accounted for by a simple relative price change. Of course, it would be wrong to attribute all the changes in manufacturing import shares to specific policies. The behaviour of the share of the rest of the world group shows that the stage of development of economies was also having an important effect. Although we have focused on manufacturing imports, the results for food and raw materials are informative. As expected, the impact of devaluation was clearest in raw material imports but the changes in shares were smaller than those observed for manufacturing and food. In any case the results for food and raw materials should be seen as tentative. Imports of these commodities are less likely to respond to policy changes; domestic import substitution is limited by resource availability and trade substitution between trading groups is likely to be similarly constrained. Furthermore the internal demand for such commodities, particularly raw materials, will be influenced by the process off economic growth in the exporting countries.

Conclusions

The evidence presented in this chapter shows that the General Tariff was important in explaining the falling import propensity of the manufacturing sector in the UK. Devaluation was of secondary importance. The evidence on import and export competitiveness shows that the largest changes were observed in import competitiveness, as a result of the General Tariff. Estimates of manufacturing import functions show that the tariff elasticity is significantly higher than the non-tariff price elasticity. The comparison of import sources also shows that, in the case of manufactured goods, tariffs

Table 4.10 Ordinary least squares trends in the shares of UK raw material imports, current prices (t-statistics in parenthesis)

Trading bloc	Annual % change		Inter-period trend differences
	(1)	(2)	
	Trend coefficients for 1924–31	Trend coefficients for 1931–7	
British countries	0.41 (1.62)	1.20 (9.61)*	1.20
Gold bloc	0.40 (2.62)*	−0.73 −(0.40)	−0.40
Core competitors	−1.63 −(3.83)*	−0.66 −(1.60)	1.63
Non-British trade agreement countries	0.55 (2.33)*	−0.02 −(0.23)	−0.55
Rest of the world	0.27 (0.72)	−0.32 −(1.25)	0.00

Notes:
*Significant at 95 per cent confidence level (one-tailed test).
Where the t-statistic is not significant we take the actual value of the coefficient to be equal to zero.

were the most important variable in explaining the changing shares of different blocs. A devaluation effect was only discernible in the case of food and raw material imports.

Appendix 4.1: The calculation of the average manufacturing tariff rate in 1932

The calculation of the tariff rate is complicated by the diverse rate structure and coverage of the legislation. An average rate of 13.2 per cent for manufactures has been calculated using the data published in Leak (1937). Applying the coverage of the Import Duties Act to imports in 1936 Leak presents the following categorisation of manufacturing imports for 1930 (Leak, 1937, appendix III, p. 593):

	£ millions
Exempt from duty	22.5
Import Duties Act/Ottawa	200.2
Silk and artificial silk	27.0
McKenna	10.1
Key industry	2.3
Hydrocarbon oils	43.3
Other duties	1.4
Total	£306.8

Since our aim is to calculate the average rate of duty for manufacturing subject to the policy change of 1932 we have excluded hydrocarbon oils from our calculations. Leak (1937, p. 587) also suggests that approximately 11 per cent of the second group (Import Duties Act/Ottawa) came in duty free through the Ottawa agreements. This leaves £178.2m of imports subject to the Import Duties Act. Leak gives details of the rates of duty in force in 1933/4 which would have been applied to 1930 imports dutiable under the Import Duties Act. Assuming that the distribution of duties was representative of all dutiable imports, the following distribution of rates

Rate of duty %	Per cent of imports
10	28.1
15	8.7
20	41.8
25	4.8
30	3.1
33.3	12.3
50	1.2
Total	100.0

Table A4.1 *Average tariff rates for manufactures under the Import Duties Act 1932–1937*

	Average tariff from Leak (Including hydrocarbon oils)	Manufacturing average tariff rate
1932	17.2	13.2
1933	18.5	14.1
1934	19.4	14.8
1935	19.3	14.7
1936	19.3	14.7
1937	19.3	14.7

would have applied: This gives an average duty of 19.3 per cent on manufactures paying duty under the Import Duties Act. On all manufactures (excluding hydrocarbon oils) an average rate of 13.2 per cent is applicable. This assumes that the goods exempt from duty were all manufactures – although many of the goods (such as essential oils) would not now be classified as such. Thus the rate of 13.2 per cent is a lower bound.

It should also be noted that the distribution of rates is based on duties applicable in 1933–4. Subsequent changes in duties, including the increased use of specific rates, tended to raise the incidence of the tariff in subsequent years. As a means of calculating a time series of average tariff rates for manufactures subject to the Import Duties Act we have assumed that the *proportion* between our figure of 13.2 and Leak's figure of 17.2 for 1932 holds for the other years. Hence we have adjusted Leak's figures accordingly in table A4.1.

5   Industrial performance and trade policy: a disaggregated analysis

Introduction

The discriminatory nature of protectionism means that a process of import substitution is likely to result from such policies. Thus, on *a priori* grounds the newly protected industries of 1932 should have received a favourable stimulus, improving their standing relative to the non-protected and already protected industries. Most of the existing literature on the impact of the 1932 tariff has in fact focused on the issue of import substitution. In this chapter we present an extensive re-evaluation of the disaggregated evidence.

A study of the sectoral impact of the General Tariff is needed not only in terms of resolving some of the problems arising from the existing literature, but as a way of checking the reliability of the macroeconomic argument and evidence presented in chapter 4. The existence of a well-defined sector subject to the policy change of 1932 allows us a further test of the claim that much of the fall in import propensities was due to tariffs. Moreover, we are not arguing that the General Tariff was the only influence on sectoral growth performance; a disaggregated analysis is necessary to distinguish the characteristics of those industries that benefited most from protection from those that benefited least. Two levels of industrial disaggregation will be used in this chapter. A broad industrial classification will be used to analyse the role of changes in trade in accounting for sectoral growth performance. At this level we have assembled a continuous data set for eleven industries which allows us to consider import propensities, export performance, output, employment and productivity. Unfortunately the complexity of the tariff regulations means that this data set is not at a level of disaggregation which would allow us to compare the newly protected with non-newly protected industries.[1] For this analysis we used the information found in the Censuses of Production for the years 1924, 1930 and 1935. Although this information only allows for benchmark comparisons between these dates, the finer level of disaggregation makes it possible to distinguish the newly protected industries[2] from other industries.

Sectoral growth performance and trade performance

In chapter 1 we noted the importance of the idea of relative trend improvement for understanding the nature of economic revival in the 1930s. The economic recovery of 1932–7 should best be viewed both as a cyclical and a relative trend revival. As a starting point, in this chapter we shall use the industrial classification of Lomax (1959) to distinguish the industries accounting for the observed relative trend improvement in aggregate industrial performance. In table 5.1a we present various descriptive statistics for a number of manufacturing industries experiencing improved performance in the 1930s. The inter-period growth comparisons between 1900–29 and 1929–37 or 1913–29 and 1929–37 show relative trend improvement in chemicals, metal manufactures, electrical engineering, textiles, leather, clothing and food, drink and tobacco. Mechanical engineering, shipbuilding, timber, paper and printing, mining and quarrying and building and contracting show either deteriorating long-term performance in the 1930s or an overall performance comparable to the pre-1929 sectoral growth trends (see table 5.1b).

From such a level of disaggregation we cannot distinguish the effect of the tariff from other influences. Some sectors subject to the General Tariff of 1932 performed relatively well (such as textiles and metal manufactures) but so did sectors not subject to the policy change (such as food, drink and tobacco). However, this level of disaggregation does allow us to show to what extent the relative trend improvement of the 1930s was correlated with trade policy induced changes. We have examined this relationship by looking at a sectoral decomposition of the Harrod multiplier. At a disaggregated level the Harrod multiplier can be specified as:

$$g_{Qi} = \frac{g_{xi}}{m_i} \tag{1}$$

$i = 1, \ldots, n$ sectors

$g_{Qi} = $ growth of industry i output

$g_{xi} = $ growth of industry i exports

$m_i = $ industry i import propensity

Equation (1) can be decomposed into the following comparative static changes:

$$\Delta g_{Qi} = \frac{1}{m_i} \Delta g_{xi} + g_{xi} \Delta \left(\frac{1}{m_i} \right) \tag{2}$$

Table 5.1a *Peak to peak growth rates for industries showing relative trend improvement 1900–1937 (% growth per annum)*

Industry	Peak to peak years	Output growth rate	Inter-period growth change
Chemicals	1900–7	3.79	—
	1907–13	2.17	−1.62
	1913–25	0.59	−1.58
	1925–9	3.74	3.15
	1929–37	3.52	−0.22
	1900–29	2.12	—
	1929–37	3.52	1.40
	1913–29	1.38	—
	1929–37	3.52	2.14
Metal manufactures	1900–7	2.06	—
	1907–13	2.37	0.31
	1913–25	−0.74	−3.11
	1925–9	3.45	4.19
	1929–37	4.53	1.08
	1900–29	1.16	—
	1929–37	4.53	3.37
	1913–29	0.31	—
	1929–37	4.53	4.22
Textiles	1900–7	2.88	—
	1907–13	1.91	−0.97
	1913–25	−1.69	−3.60
	1925–9	−0.87	0.82
	1929–37	3.05	3.92
	1900–29	0.27	—
	1929–37	3.05	2.78
	1913–29	−1.48	—
	1929–37	3.05	4.53
Food, drink and tobacco	1900–7	1.24	—
	1907–13	2.11	0.87
	1913–25	−1.02	−3.13
	1925–9	2.32	3.34
	1929–37	2.95	0.63

Table 5.1a *contd.*

Industry	Peak to peak years	Output growth rate	Inter-period growth change
	1900–29	1.36	—
	1929–37	2.95	1.59
	1913–29	1.13	—
	1929–37	2.95	1.82
Electrical engineering	1900–7	6.20	—
	1907–13	6.29	0.09
	1913–25	4.68	−1.61
	1925–9	1.50	−3.10
	1929–37	7.50	6.00
	1900–29	4.94	—
	1929–37	7.50	2.56
	1913–29	3.88	—
	1929–37	7.50	3.62
Leather	1900–7	−2.73	—
	1907–13	1.88	4.61
	1913–25	0.86	−1.02
	1925–9	−1.22	−2.08
	1929–37	3.61	4.83
	1900–29	−0.83	—
	1929–37	3.61	4.44
	1913–29	0.34	—
	1929–37	3.61	3.27
Clothing	1900–7	0.48	—
	1907–13	1.26	0.78
	1913–25	−1.02	−2.28
	1925–9	2.49	3.51
	1929–37	1.73	−0.76
	1900–29	0.30	—
	1929–37	1.73	1.43
	1913–29	−0.15	—
	1929–37	1.73	1.88

Source: The industrial production data are from Lomax (1959).

Table 5.1b *Peak to peak growth rates for industries not showing relative trend improvement 1900–1937 (% growth per annum)*

Industry	Peak to peak years	Output growth rate	Inter-period growth change
Mechanical engineering	1900–7	−0.33	—
	1907–13	3.20	3.53
	1913–25	0.85	−2.35
	1925–9	1.47	0.62
	1929–37	0.71	−0.76
	1900–29	1.11	—
	1929–37	0.71	−0.40
	1913–29	1.00	—
	1929–37	0.71	−0.29
Shipbuilding	1900–7	1.76	—
	1907–13	3.49	1.73
	1913–25	−6.69	−10.18
	1925–9	1.12	7.81
	1929–37	0.87	−0.25
	1900–29	−0.07	—
	1929–37	0.87	0.94
	1913–29	−2.21	—
	1929–37	0.87	3.08
Timber	1900–7	−0.77	—
	1907–13	0.29	1.06
	1913–25	1.85	1.56
	1925–9	7.13	5.28
	1929–37	3.23	−3.90
	1900–29	1.62	—
	1929–37	3.23	1.61
	1913–29	3.17	—
	1929–37	3.23	0.06
Paper and printing	1900–7	3.06	—
	1907–13	3.44	0.38
	1913–25	2.62	−0.82
	1925–9	3.32	0.70
	1929–37	2.53	−0.79

Table 5.1b *contd.*

Industry	Peak to peak years	Output growth rate	Inter-period growth change
	1900–29	2.99	—
	1929–37	2.53	−0.46
	1913–29	2.80	—
	1929–37	2.53	−0.27
Mining and quarrying	1900–7	2.28	—
	1907–13	0.87	−1.41
	1913–25	−1.19	−2.06
	1925–9	1.80	2.99
	1929–37	−0.48	−2.28
	1900–29	0.49	—
	1929–37	0.48	−0.97
	1913–29	−0.44	—
	1929–37	−0.48	−0.04
Building and contracting	1900–7	−3.02	—
	1907–13	−5.19	−2.17
	1913–25	5.76	10.95
	1925–9	2.69	−3.07
	1929–37	2.89	0.20
	1900–29	0.95	—
	1929–37	2.89	1.94
	1913–29	4.99	—
	1929–37	2.89	−2.10

Source: Data for industrial production are from Lomax (1959)

Thus, variations in the growth of output are caused by two effects:
(1) variations in the growth of exports; and
(2) variations in the magnitude of the foreign trade multiplier.* The latter effect will be taken as being induced by changes in trade policy, tariffs and devaluation combined.[3] We attempted to quantify these effects using disaggregated cross sectional data for a number of subperiods.

*The second order effects are assumed to be small.

Table 5.2 presents the descriptive statistics relating to equation (2) above. The pattern of growth rate changes suggests a fairly strong correlation with changes in the foreign trade multiplier but a weak correlation with export growth changes. The correlation coefficient for the output growth changes between 1900–29 and 1929–37 and the Harrod multiplier changes is 0.51 while the correlation coefficient with export growth changes is only 0.02. For the inter-period comparisons of 1913–29 and 1929–37 the two correlations are 0.85 and 0.17 respectively. As a way of testing the statistical significance of these relationships we estimated equation (2) using regression analysis.[4] For the period 1900–37 we obtained the following results ('t' values in parentheses):

$$\Delta g_{Qi} = -0.10189 \; \Delta g_{xi} + 0.39716 \; \Delta \left(\frac{1}{m_i}\right)$$
$$\phantom{\Delta g_{Qi} =} -(1.2) (2.63)$$

For the period 1913–37 the equation estimated is:

$$\Delta g_{Qi} = -0.03053 \; \Delta g_{xi} + 0.65737 \; \Delta \left(\frac{1}{m_i}\right)$$
$$\phantom{\Delta g_{Qi} =} -(0.57) (5.97)$$

Thus, in both subperiods the only statistically significant variable is the change in the magnitude of the Harrod foreign trade multiplier.[5]

The evidence presented in this section suggests that trade policies were important to explaining the relative performance of industries in the 1930s. However, at this stage we cannot distinguish the effect of tariffs from other influences.

The relative performance of the newly protected industries of 1932

The data contained in the Censuses of Production of 1924, 1930 and 1935 (HMSO, 1930–2, 1933–5, 1938–44) are at a sufficient level of disaggregation to allow us to distinguish the performance of the newly protected industries of 1932 relative to other industries. In using the information in the Censuses of Production[6] we are following the approach of Richardson (1967). However, instead of comparing the relative position of the newly protected industries only for the years 1930 and 1935 we use the benchmark comparisons of 1924, 1930 and 1935 as a way of capturing relative performance in the light of the initial conditions faced by different industries before the policy shift in 1932. Thus, the inter-period differences

Table 5.2 *A decomposition of the Harrod foreign trade multiplier on a sectoral basis*

Industry ($i = 1-11$)	(1) $\Delta \bar{g}_{yi}(\%)$	(2) $\Delta \bar{g}_{yi}(\%)$	(3) $\Delta\left(\dfrac{1}{m_i}\right)$	(4) $\Delta \bar{g}_{xi}(\%)$
Chemicals	1.40	2.14	4.05	−4.70
Iron and steel	3.52	4.60	5.42	−7.96
Textiles	2.77	4.53	7.83	−3.97
Electrical engineering	2.56	3.62	3.58	−5.76
Leather	4.44	3.27	1.12	−1.89
Clothing	1.43	1.87	3.38	−4.13
Timber	1.62	0.06	−0.32	−14.85
Paper	−0.46	−0.27	−0.72	−3.75
Mechanical engineering	−0.42	−0.29	0.36	−6.72
Metal goods	0.95	0.95	1.53	0.58
Vehicles	0.84	0.84	19.52	−13.98

Notes:
Column (1) Measures trend improvement between the years 1929–37 and 1900–29. The exceptions are metal goods and vehicles where data limitations only allow for a comparison of 1924–9 and 1929–37.
Column (2) Measures trend improvement between the years 1929–37 and 1913–29. Metal goods and vehicles are measured as for column 1.
Column (3) Measures the change in the Harrod foreign trade multiplier for different sectors. The numbers are absolute changes not percentage changes. The years for comparison are 1929–37 and 1924–9.
Column (4) Measures the change in export growth for the periods 1929–37 and 1924–9.
Sources: Lomax (1969) and Board of Trade (annual).

in performance between 1924–30 and 1930–5 are the relevant measure of the possible effects of protection on different industries.[7]

The import duties of 1931–2 covered the majority of manufacturing industry, accounting for some 88 per cent of output. Most of the remaining industries had been protected under earlier legislation, including motor cars, scientific instruments and synthetic chemicals (see appendix 5.1 for full details of protected industries). On *a priori* grounds the newly protected industries would benefit from the imposition of import duties, generating an import substitution effect for the economy as a whole. In order to test whether such differentiated sectoral effects were observed we examined the relative performance of the newly protected industries with respect to trade

performance, import penetration, output growth, employment and productivity.[8]

The initial impact of protection would be expected to be on trade
performance. The relative values for imports and exports for the two sectors
(newly protected and non-newly protected) are presented in table 5.3.
Looking at the value of imports[9] it is clear that the two sectors saw very
different initial conditions during 1924–30; while the newly protected sector
of 1932 saw a rise in the value of imports of 0.5 per cent per annum the
other industries saw a fall of 1.35 per cent per annum. During 1930–5 both
sectors saw a substantial decline in the value of imports. However, the
inter-period comparisons suggest a much larger trend reversal for the newly
protected sector than the other sector.[10] The initial conditions for the two
sectors also differed substantially in terms of export performance. During
1924–30 the newly protected sector of 1932 saw an annual fall in exports of
7.9 per cent while the other sector saw an increase of 0.2 per cent. In the
period 1930–5 both sectors suffered a substantial decline in the value of
their exports of 5.1 per cent and 4.8 per cent per annum respectively.[11]
Allowing for the differing initial conditions the inter-period growth
comparisons suggest a relative improvement for the newly protected sector
and a relative deterioration for the other industries.

The trends in import penetration[12] for the two sectors are shown in table
5.4. As with import values, import penetration for both sectors shows
a substantial fall during 1930–5, with a larger fall being observed for the
newly protected sector. The nature of the change for the newly protected
sector is even more striking given the different paths of the two sectors
during the 1924–30 period. While the newly protected sector of 1932 saw an
increase in import propensity during the 1920s the other sector saw a fall.
Hence, in terms of inter-period trend comparisons the newly protected
sector saw a fall in import propensity almost double that of the other sector.

Within our analysis of the impact of the tariff we would expect that
a policy induced fall in import penetration would stimulate import
substitution in the protected industries. In addition there would be
macroeconomic effects that would affect the other industries and, hence,
generate further repercussion effects on the protected industries. Output
growth in the newly protected group of 1932 was stagnant between 1924
and 1930 whilst the other sector saw a respectable growth of 2.7 per cent per
annum (see table 5.5).[13] However, during 1930–5 there occurred a substantial turnaround, the newly protected group grew at 3.8 per cent per
annum whilst the other industries grew at 2.3 per cent per annum. The
inter-period growth comparisons illustrate this turnaround in performance
clearly.[14] The impact of the policy shift on employment and productivity in
the two sectors is shown in table 5.6. Employment in the newly protected
industries increased at an annual rate of 1.1 per cent between 1930 and 1935

Table 5.3 *Retained imports and exports for the newly protected and non-newly protected manufacturing sectors (current prices)*

	Newly protected	Non-newly protected
Imports: level of retained imports (£)		
1924	201579	132348
1930	207683	121957
1935	128433	81424
Growth per annum (%)		
1924–30	0.50	− 1.35
1930–5	− 9.16	− 7.76
Inter-period growth differences (%)		
1924–30 and		
1930–5	− 9.66	− 6.41
Exports: level of exports (£)		
1924	515488	90309
1930	314253	91420
1935	251702	71339
Growth per annum (%)		
1924–30	− 7.92	0.20
1930–5	− 5.11	− 4.84
Inter-period growth differences (%)		
1924–30 and		
1930–5	2.81	− 5.04

Table 5.4 *Import penetration for the newly protected and non-newly protected manufacturing sectors (current prices)*

	Newly protected (%)	Non-newly protected (%)
1924	13.6	22.3
1930	15.8	20.1
1935	9.1	12.7
Growth per annum (%)		
1924–30	2.5	− 1.7
1930–5	− 10.4	− 8.8
Inter period growth differences (%)		
1924–30 and		
1930–5	− 12.9	− 7.1

Table 5.5 *Output levels and growth rates for the newly protected and non-newly protected manufacturing sectors* (1935 = 100)

	Newly protected	Non-newly protected
1924	83.22	76.13
1930	82.83	89.18
1935	100.00	100.00
Growth per annum (%)		
1924–30	−0.1	2.7
1930–5	3.8	2.3
Inter-period growth differences (%) 1924–30 and		
1930–5	3.9	−0.4

Table 5.6 *Employment and productivity for the newly protected and non-newly protected manufacturing sectors*

	Newly protected	Non-newly protected
Employment		
1924	3492117	896518
1930	3383519	964387
1935	3572282	1006057
Growth per annum (%)		
1924–30	−0.53	1.22
1930–5	1.09	0.85
Inter-period growth differences (%) 1924–30 and		
1930–5	1.62	−0.37
Productivity		
1924	85.1	85.4
1930	87.4	93.0
1935	100.0	100.0
Growth per annum (%)		
1924–30	0.45	1.43
1930–5	2.73	1.46
Inter-period growth differences (%) 1924–30 and		
1930–5	2.28	0.03

compared to negative growth in the 1920s. In the non-newly protected group the growth of employment between 1930 and 1935 actually retarded relative to the 1920s.[15] The productivity path of the two sectors also shows a major turnaround in the 1930s, with the newly protected sector showing a significant improvement in performance.

The evidence presented in this disaggregated analysis shows an improved performance of the newly protected industries relative to other manufacturing industries, supporting the idea that tariffs in the 1930s generated a successful process of import substitution.

The characteristics of manufacturing industries and the impact of tariffs

The impact of trade policies would depend on the characteristics of the different industries protected in 1932. As a way of distinguishing the characteristics of industries benefiting most from the General Tariff we employ the classification scheme of the OECD (1987), which groups industries according to the primary factor which affects competitiveness in each activity. Industries are grouped into one of four categories: resources intensive, labour intensive, scale intensive or differentiated products (see appendix 5.1). In classifying protected and non-protected industries in this way we will get an insight into the processes by which trade policies may affect competitiveness.[16]

Table 5.7 shows that labour intensive industries saw an inter-period annual growth improvement of 6.0 per cent. The vast majority of this sector consisted of newly protected industries, including most of the clothing and textile trades. The only major labour intensive activity that was not newly protected was the silk industry which was protected by previous legislation. The primary factor affecting competitiveness in the labour intensive activities is labour costs. While a tariff cannot directly affect labour costs it can decrease the relative price of the domestic product, generating improved competitiveness. For this improvement to be sustained there must be a sufficient supply of labour to prevent a large increase in own product real wages sufficient to neutralise the competitive effect of the tariff. The labour intensive activities had suffered a decline in activity during the 1920s with a substantial fall in employment. Moreover, the labour that was shed was not absorbed by other industries due to the low level of overall economic activity, particularly in those regions in which these activities were concentrated. As pointed out in chapter 1 real wage pressure was not a serious problem in the recovery period.

Scale intensive industries also show a substantial improvement in performance (see table 5.8). The inter-period comparisons show an overall annual growth rate improvement of 1.4 per cent. The comparisons between the newly protected industries and the others suggest that most of the

Table 5.7 *Output levels and growth rates of labour intensive industries* (*1935 = 100*)

	All labour intensive industries	
Output levels		
1924	88.74	
1930	80.57	
1935	100.00	
Growth per annum (%)		
1924–30	−1.6	
1930–5	4.4	
Inter-period growth differences (%)		
1924–30 and		
1930–5	6.0	
	Newly protected[1]	Non-newly protected[2]
Output levels		
1924	92.01	26.79
1930	82.07	47.00
1935	100.00	100.00
Growth per annum (%)		
1924–30	−1.9	9.8
1930–5	4.0	16.3
Inter-period growth differences (%)		
1924–30 and		
1930–5	5.9	6.5

Notes:

[1] Number of industries in this category is 21.

[2] Number of industries in this category is only 3.

improvement can be attributed to the former. The inter-period comparisons for the newly protected group show an improvement of 2.9 per cent per annum compared with 0.2 per cent for the already protected industries. The superior performance of the newly protected group might have been due to the outlier of shipbuilding in the non-newly protected group. This industry exhibited rapid decline throughout the 1920s and 1930s due to excess world supply, often facilitated by protectionism. However, even if shipbuilding is removed from the non-newly protected group the increase in the annual growth rate of 2.1 per cent still does not match that of the newly protected group.

Table 5.8 *Output levels and growth rates of scale intensive industries*
(1935 = 100)

	All scale intensive industries
Output levels	
1924	79.25
1930	86.55
1935	100.00
Growth per annum (%)	
1924–30	1.5
1930–5	2.9
Inter-period growth differences (%)	
1924–30 and	
1930–5	1.4

	Newly protected[1]	Non-newly protected[2]
Output levels		
1924	80.45	78.21
1930	83.84	88.87
1935	100.00	100.00
Growth per annum (%)		
1924–30	0.7	2.2
1930–5	3.6	2.4
Inter-period growth differences (%)		
1924–30 and		
1930–5	2.9	0.2

Notes:
[1] Number of industries in this category is 19.
[2] Number of industries in this category is 14.

The principal factor affecting competitiveness in the scale intensive industries was the level of activity. Thus any initial competitive advantage afforded by a tariff could become self sustaining. The initial process of import substitution would lead to the increased utilisation of plant, the lengthening of production runs and the reduction of unit costs. The process depends initially on producers not raising domestic prices to offset the benefit of the tariff. If this happened there would be no output effect, but a redistribution of income to domestic producers. However, the evidence of Leak (1937) suggests that many producers responded to the tariff by reducing prices. The second necessary condition is the existence of excess

Table 5.9 *Output levels and growth rates of industries producing differentiated products* (1935 = 100)

	All differentiated products	
Output levels		
1924	80.46	
1930	88.81	
1935	100.00	
Growth per annum (%)		
1924–30	1.7	
1930–5	2.4	
Inter-period growth differences (%)		
1924–30 and		
1930–5	+0.7	

	Newly protected[1]	Non-newly protected[2]	
Output levels			
1924	79.05	59.93	49.43
1930	84.17	126.46	65.54
1935	100.00	100.00	100.00
Growth per annum (%)			
1924	1.1	13.3	4.8
1930	3.5	−4.6	8.8
Inter-period growth differences (%)			
1924–30 and			
1930–5	2.4	−17.9	4.0

Notes:
[1] Number of industries in this category is 9.
[2] Number of industries in this category is 7 in the first column and 6 in the second column (excluding musical instruments).

capacity. The low level of activity, particularly following the recession of 1929–32, created a pool of under-utilised resources. Moreover the initial expansion of activity following the imposition of the tariff combined with the prevailing monetary policy encouraged increased investment in new plant and machinery.

Table 5.9 presents the results for differentiated products. It is in these groups that specialisation is most important and the potential gains from trade are most apparent. The overall improvement of these industries between 1924–30 and 1930–5 was only 0.7 per cent per annum. Although

Table 5.10 *Output levels and growth rates of raw material based industries* $(1935 = 100)$

	All raw material based industries
Output levels	
1924	78.20
1930	87.41
1935	100.00
Growth per annum (%)	
1924–30	1.9
1930–5	2.7
Inter-period growth differences (%)	
1924–30 and	
1930–5	0.8

	Newly protected[1]	Non-newly protected[2]
Output levels		
1924	69.74	80.77
1930	79.91	89.70
1935	100.00	100.00
Growth per annum (%)		
1924–30	2.3	1.8
1930–5	4.6	2.2
Inter-period growth differences (%)		
1924–30 and		
1930–5	2.3	0.4

Notes:
[1] Number of industries in this category is 13.
[2] Number of industries in this category is 23.

the newly protected industries saw an improvement of 2.4 per cent per annum in the two periods, a relevant comparison with the non-newly protected industries is not possible because of the small sample for the latter; the performance of this group varies significantly depending on the inclusion of different industries (see table 5.9).

Competitiveness in differentiated products depends on demand and the ability to supply specialist products. The introduction of a tariff therefore is unlikely to bring about a substantial benefit for this sector. In particular the process of import substitution will be limited if domestic producers are unable to provide similar goods to those imported. Thus the expansion of this sector will depend on its ability to reorganise production in response to the changing pattern of demand induced through protection, thereby specialising in new products. Such reorganisation will take time and depend on the level of specialisation and technology required.

The final group of activities are those that are resource intensive.[17] Table 5.10 shows that the overall growth performance of these industries improved by only 0.8 per cent per annum between the 1924–30 and 1930–5 periods. The performance of the newly protected group improved by 2.3 per cent and the non-newly protected group by 0.4 per cent. Despite the s..ghtly better performance of the newly protected group the impact of the tariff on these activities was limited. The main factor affecting competitiveness in this group is access to natural resources. The tariff, by raising import prices, would have encouraged the exploitation of domestic resources. Many of the activities in this group, however, were dependent on imported resources and thus the impact of devaluation would have been to make input prices higher than they would otherwise have been.

The disaggregated evidence presented in this section suggests that the import substitution process was strongest in the labour intensive and scale intensive industries. The effects of protection were much weaker for resource intensive activities and sectors producing differentiated products. However, given the large weight of the scale and labour intensive industries in the interwar period the tariff had a large net beneficial effect on the protected sector and the economy as a whole.

Conclusions

The evidence presented in this chapter has shown that the UK economy underwent a successful process of import substitution following the imposition of the General Tariff of 1932. The study of Richardson (1967) generated erroneous conclusions by neglecting the initial conditions faced by different industries in the 1920s. Although the level of disaggregation of this study does not allow us to look at the concept of effective protection, the disaggregated evidence of a favourable tariff effect in 1932 raises serious doubts as to the predictive power of Capie's (1978, 1983) evidence for the 1930s.[18] Finally, the effect of protection was most favourable to scale intensive and labour intensive industries. Given the predominance of these industries in the interwar UK economy the net effect of the tariff on revival in the period of 1932–7 was significant. Similarly the increasing importance of differentiated and science-based products in the modern British economy would reduce the effect of any protectionist policy today.

Appendix 5.1 Industrial classification

Index: A = Newly protected in 1932
       B = Non-newly protected in 1932
       1 = Resource intensive industries
       2 = Labour intensive industries
       3 = Scale intensive industries
       4 = Differentiated products

Industry	Protection group	Activity type
Textile trades		
cotton spinning	A	2
cotton weaving	A	2
woollen and worsted	A	2
silk and artificial silk	B	2
linen and hemp	A	2
jute	A	2
hosiery	A	2
textile finishing	A	2
lace	B	2
rope twine nets	A	2
elastic webbing	A	2
coir fibre etc.	A	2
flock and rag	A	2
packing	A	2
canvas good sack	A	2
engine boiler packing	A	2
roofing felts	A	2
Clothing trades		
tailoring and dressmaking	A	2
boot and shoe	A	2
hat and cap	A	2
glove	B	2
umbrella	A	2
fur	A	1
Iron and steel trades		
blast furnaces	A	3
smelting and rolling	A	3
foundries	A	3
tinplate	A	3
wrought iron and steel	A	3
wire	A	3
chain nail and screw	A	3

Appendix 5.1 *contd.*

Industry	Protection group	Activity type
hardware and holloware	A	3
cutlery	B	4
tools and implements	A	4
needle pin smallwares	A	4
small arms	A	4
Engineering, shipbuilding and vehicles trades		
mechanical engineering	A	4
electrical engineering	A	4
shipbuilding	B	3
motor and cycle	B	3
aircraft	A	3
railway carriage and wagon	A	3
carriage cart and wagon	A	3
Non-ferrous metals		
copper and brass	A	1
aluminium, lead and tin	A	1
finished brass	A	1
gold and silver	B	1
plate and jewellery	A	4
watch and clock	B	4
Chemical trades		
chemical dyes and drugs	B	3
seed crushing	B	3
oil and tallow	B	3
fertiliser disinfectant glue	B	3
soap candle perfume	B	3
starch polishes	A	3
paint colour varnishes	A	3
explosives	B	3
match	B	3
ink gum wax	B	3
petroleum	B	1
Leather trades		
fellmongery	A	1
leather tanning	A	1
leather goods	A	1
Paper, printing and stationery trades		
paper	B	1
wallpaper	A	3

Appendix 5.1 *contd.*

Industry	Protection group	Activity type
printing and books	A	3
print and publish newspapers	B	3
manufactured stationery	A	3
cardboard box	A	3
pens and pencils	A	3
Miscellaneous trades		
rubber	B	3
linoleum and oilcloth	A	3
musical instrument	B	4
games and toys	B	4
sports and requisites	A	4
scientific instruments	B	4
film printing	B	4
incandescent mantles	A	4
fancy goods	B	4
coke and coke by-product	B	1
manufactured fuel	B	1
brush	A	4
manufactured abrasives	A	1
Timber trades		
timber	A	1
furniture	A	2
wooden crates and boxes	A	1
coopering	A	2
cane and wicker	A	1
Clay and building materials		
brick and fireclay	A	1
china and earthenware	B	3
glass	B	3
cement	B	1
building materials	A	1

Appendix 5.2 Significance tests for differences in output performance between the newly protected and non-newly protected industries

In order to test the statistical significance of the differences in growth performance between the two sectors we have undertaken *t*-tests on the differences in the two sample means. Similar tests were also used to test the differences in growth over the

two periods 1924–30 and 1930–5. These tests require that the following conditions are satisfied:
  (i) the observations are independent,
 (ii) the variances of the two samples are equal, and
(iii) the observations are normally distributed.
Condition (i) is not a serious problem here since the sample is cross-sectional; condition (ii) is not satisfied when we compare the newly protected and non-newly protected industries. In these cases we have used an adjusted t-test that recognises the reduced degrees of freedom. Condition (iii) is likely to be satisfied for the reasonably large cross-sectional samples we are working with.
   The output growth rate of two classes of industries can be defined as:

$$g_{jt} = \frac{\sum\limits_{i=1}^{n} X_{it} W_i}{\sum\limits_{i=1}^{n} X_{it-1} W_i} \tag{1}$$

$j = 1, 2$ (1 = newly protected; 2 = non-newly protected)
$i = 1, \ldots, n$
X_i = Volume of production of industry i
W_i = Weight of industry i, measured as net output of industry i in 1930 as a proportion of total net output in 1930

For the significance test we have used a logarithmic approximation of equation (1),

$$G_{jt} = \sum_{i=1}^{n} W_i \Delta \log X_{it} \tag{2}$$

From equation (2) the percentage total growth over the two periods 1924–30 and 1930–5 for the two groups of industries are:

	Newly protected	*Non-newly protected*
1924–30	2.46	21.81
1930–5	19.63	18.78

The following significance tests were undertaken:
  (i) For the newly protected group (a sample of sixty-two industries) we tested the null hypothesis that the mean growth over the two periods is equal. The value of the t-statistic is 3.17 rejecting the null at the 99 per cent confidence level. The mean growth of the newly protected industries was thus significantly improved in the 1930–5 period.
 (ii) A similar test was undertaken for the non-newly protected group (a sample of thirty industries). The value of the t-statistic is 0.39 failing to reject the null hypothesis that the mean growth of the periods 1924–30 and 1930–5 were equal.
(iii) Finally we tested the null hypothesis that the mean growth of the newly protected and non-newly protected groups (a total sample of ninety-two) was equal in the two subperiods. Given that the variances for the two samples are different we used an adjusted t-test. For the period 1924–30 the adjusted t-test

on the differences between the two means was 2.47, rejecting the null hypothesis of equal means at the 99 per cent confidence level. However in the 1930–5 period the adjusted t-statistic is 0.79 failing to reject the null hypothesis of equal means for the two types of industries. Thus, while the newly protected industries grew significantly slower than the others between 1924 and 1930, their average performance was equal to the non-newly protected industries during 1930–5.

6 The 1930s economic revival: an overview

Introduction

There are two broad questions that need to be addressed with respect to understanding the economic revival in the 1930s; first, why did the economy see a turning point in its cyclical behaviour in the third quarter of 1932 and secondly, why did the economy traverse onto a path of relative trend improvement in economic growth?[1] In this chapter we place the contribution of protectionism in this overall context, arguing that the imposition of tariffs contributed both to the turning point and the long-term change of the economy. We must stress that tariffs by themselves provide an incomplete explanation of revival in the 1930s; it is important to recognise the impact of other influences on the recovery. In general, discussions of recovery during the period have been structured around the theme of a 'natural recovery', emphasising endogenous cyclical mechanisms, explanation versus a policy induced explanation. In this chapter we follow this presentational schema.

Other policy initiatives

Devaluation

We have already mentioned the contributory effect of devaluation in helping to reduce the import propensity of the economy, providing a small competitive boost that lasted throughout 1932–7. The various exchange rate indicators suggest that the competitive advantage was particularly large in 1932 (see table 4.2 and figure 4.3). Taking Redmond's (1980) figure of a 13 per cent depreciation during 1931–2 Broadberry (1986) undertook an elasticities analysis of the policy change. Since the empirical evidence suggests that the Marshall-Lerner condition was satisfied, Broadberry calculated that the improvement in the balance of trade, resulting from this competitive advantage, amounted to £80m.[2] Assuming a multiplier of 1.75 this gives a total effect of GDP of 3 per cent, accounting for a large part of the turning point in 1932.

Such quantification of the impact of depreciation is clearly an over-estimate in the circumstances of the 1930s. Trade with countries whose currencies were tied to sterling accounted for one half of British exports reducing the stimulating impact of depreciation.[3] During 1931-2 the effective exchange rate for manufacturing imports from British countries only improved by about 4 per cent compared to 1929 (see table 6.1).

In the light of the absorption and monetary theories of the balance of payments the analysis of devaluation offered by a simple elasticities perspective is limited. Devaluation may generate favourable economic effects that operate through macroeconomic adjustments not directly linked to the balance of trade. In the comparative analysis of depreciation in the 1930s Eichengreen and Sachs (1985) note a statistically significant positive correlation between devaluation and economic revival for a cross-section of countries in the 1930s. The phenomenon is best explained by the fact that depreciation and flexible exchange rates enabled policy adjustment so that monetary policy could be independent of the exchange rate.[4]

Monetary policy

The depreciation of the exchange rate allowed the Government to pursue a more expansionist ('cheap money') monetary policy after 1932. Cheap money was initially a policy for reducing the size of the national debt; the Government forced interest rates down as a means of converting the war loan stock of 1917 at 5 per cent to a conversion stock at 3.5 per cent. Nevertheless, cheap money has also been seen as a permissive policy for economic revival (Richardson, 1967). The major problem faced by analysts of the effects of the cheap money policy is in documenting a convincing transmission mechanism. Although the bank rate remained at the low level of 2 per cent through 1932-9, there were no increases in bank advances to industry until 1935.[5] Nevertheless, cheap money could have stimulated recovery by stimulating consumption expenditure[6] and by its influence on the housing sector.

Two mechanisms have been emphasised with respect to the latter link. First, falling interest rates give rise to a reallocation of savings with housing investment benefiting because of the more stable returns on housing. Secondly, prior to 1932 the rate of return on building society shares was comparable to that on consols. However, the war loan conversion opened up a gap in favour of building societies; thus building societies had an excess of funds which resulted in favourable mortgage terms. The evidence is against the importance of this transmission mechanism. Building society

Table 6.1 *Effective exchange rate for manufactured imports from British countries (1929 = 100)**

1924	91.9
1925	98.7
1926	99.5
1927	99.5
1928	99.5
1929	100.0
1930	100.8
1931	102.2
1932	95.7
1933	86.9
1934	104.6
1935	103.1
1936	104.0
1937	102.7
1938	105.4

Notes:
*Countries covered are India, Canada and Australia.
Weights are average shares of UK Manufacturing trade for 1928 and 1935.
Source: Exchange rates: League of Nations, *Statistical Year Book* (various editions).
Weights: Board of Trade, *Annual Statement of Trade in the United Kingdom* (1929 and 1939).

deposits in fact grew faster in the 1920s than in the 1930s due to an increase in the proportion of savings going to building societies and also to a peak in repayments. Hence, the availability of funds in the 1930s was mainly due to the favourable conditions of the 1920s, not the monetary policy shift of 1932 (Humphries, 1987).

A number of important links remain. The fall in building society rates from 6 per cent in 1931 to 3.5 per cent in 1935 had a significant effect in lowering the cost of repayment which stimulated the demand for housing. Moreover banks provided increased funds to builders as working capital. Even if such a link between policy and the housing boom could be established, the contribution of housing to the revival of the 1930s was limited. A sectoral growth decomposition shows that the relative contribu-

Table 6.2 *The contribution to annual GDP growth by industry 1924–37*
(*% per annum*)

	1924–9	1929–32	1932–7
Agriculture	0.17	−0.03	0.03
Mining and quarrying	−0.01	−0.23	0.11
Manufacturing	0.82	−0.95	2.19
Building and contracting	0.29	−0.26	0.41
Gas, electricity and water	0.12	0.05	0.24
Transport and communications	0.24	−0.27	0.33
Distribution	0.68	0.09	1.39
GDP[1]	2.3	−1.6	4.7

Notes:
[1] Figures do not add up due to rounding.
[2] The level of disaggregation here requires use of the output measure of GDP.
Source: Feinstein (1972), T25–T27 and T112.

tion of building and contracting declined in the 1930s relative to the 1920s.
During 1924–9 this sector accounted for 12.5 per cent of the overall GDP
growth rate, a contribution which fell to 8.7 per cent during 1932–7 (see
table 6.2). In contrast manufacturing industries accounted for 35.6 per cent
and 46.6 per cent of the GDP growth rate in the two periods respectively,
which suggests that it was this *sector* which played the dominant role in the
acceleration of the overall rate of growth after 1932.[7]

This is not to deny the critical role of housing in the early stages of
recovery. Although housing accounted for only 3 per cent of GDP it
accounted for 17 per cent of the *change* in GDP between 1932 and 1934; in
terms of employment, building accounted for 7.5 per cent of total
employment but 20 per cent of the rise in employment between 1932 and
1935 (Worswick, 1984). However, to emphasise the role of housing as
a leading sector in the early stages of recovery ignores its small contribution
to overall growth in the 1930s. Thus the existing literature has focused on
the issue of the turning point without recognising the limited role of housing
in accounting for the improved trend growth during the period.

Fiscal policy

The balanced budgets of the early 1930s have created the impression that
fiscal policy was fairly neutral in its impact on the recovery (Richardson,
1967). The traditional view also emphasised the psychological impact of
balanced budgets in contributing to the cyclical turning point of 1932. Since

the balanced budget was regarded by contemporaries as a measure of sound Government financing, the success of balancing the budget in 1931 is thought to have stimulated private investment.

These traditional interpretations have been brought into question by more recent studies of the Government's fiscal stance (Middleton, 1981). One widely used measure of fiscal stance is the constant employment budget balance (CEBB).[8] The aim of the CEBB is to measure the *ex-ante* policy initiatives of the Government, not the *ex-post* accounting balance. Let the budget surplus be defined as:

$$B_S = T - G \tag{1}$$

where T = Tax revenue, tY
$\quad\quad t$ = Marginal tax rate
$\quad\quad Y$ = Income
$\quad\quad G$ = Government expenditure

Thus:

$$B_S = tY - G \tag{2}$$

Multiplying and dividing (2) by full employment income Y^*:

$$B_S = tY^* \cdot \left(\frac{Y}{Y^*}\right) - G \tag{3}$$

Hence, the budget surplus can vary because of three influences:
   (i) a change in the tax rate, t,
  (ii) a change in capacity utilisation (Y/Y^*), and
 (iii) a change in Government expenditure, G.
The discretionary part of the budget can be evaluated by holding capacity utilisation constant and calculating the counterfactual constant employment budget balance:

$$\text{CEBB} = tY^* - G$$

Thus, the CEBB can only vary as a result of discretionary policy changes. A major cyclical downturn, as in 1929–32, will cause the *ex-post* budget surplus to deteriorate unless taxation increases and/or Government expenditure falls. The fact that the budget was balanced in 1931 suggests a deflationary fiscal stance. Middleton (1981) shows that the economy was faced with a deflationary fiscal impact of 2.5 per cent of GDP in 1931–2, rising to 3.0 per cent in 1932–3 and peaking at 4.2 per cent in 1933–4 (see table 6.3). Hence, the turning point of 1932 cannot be explained by fiscal measures in any direct way. Even if there was a favourable expectations effect from the balanced budgets of 1931–2 it would have had to be very large to compensate for the deflationary fiscal policy of the period. During 1934–8 the fiscal grip was loosened by about 1 per cent of GDP per annum,

Table 6.3 *Ex-post and constant employment budget balances 1929–40* (% *of GDP*)

	Ex-post balance[1]	Constant employment balance[2]
1929–30	+ 0.4	+ 0.4
1930–1	− 0.6	+ 1.1
1931–2	− 1.2	+ 2.5
1932–3	− 1.3	+ 3.0
1933–4	+ 0.9	+ 4.2
1934–5	+ 0.6	+ 3.2
1935–6	+ 0.4	+ 2.0
1936–7	+ 0.3	+ 0.8
1937–8	+ 0.3	0.0
1938–9	− 2.7	− 1.6
1939–40	− 13.2	− 12.2

Notes:
[1] As a % of GDP for the same year.
[2] As a % of full employment GDP, taken to be 1929 in these calculations.
Source: Middleton (1981), table 5.

providing a stimulus to the later stages of the recovery. This policy reversal was dominated by rearmament such that by 1938 the rearmament programme accounted for 30 per cent of Government expenditure.[9]

This overview of the various policy measures suggests that a number of policy initiatives may be important in accounting for the turning point of 1932. Monetary policy and depreciation each played a role in creating favourable conditions for a cyclical turning point. The favourable effects of tariffs were documented in chapters 4 and 5. In fact, only fiscal policy failed to stimulate the transition to recovery in any direct way. However, in seeking to explain the path to an improvement in relative trend growth in the 1930s the number of policy instruments capable of contributing to an explanation are reduced. The evidence presented here and in chapter 4 shows that the significant impact of devaluation was limited to a short period in 1931–3; monetary policy was favourable in the 1930s but the transmission mechanisms we have outlined do not suggest that this policy shift can account for an improvement in trend growth; fiscal policy, in the form of rearmament, contributed to sustaining the recovery after 1935 but the fiscal impact was still quite small, only compensating for the deflationary fiscal pressures of 1931–4. In contrast the imposition of tariffs on an extensive scale by Britain in 1932 represented a major policy shift. Such a change in 'system characteristics' (Maddison, 1982) could provide an explanation for the observed shift in the growth path of the economy and the sectoral aspects of recovery. In chapter 4 we showed that tariffs played a critical role in accounting for the reduction in the import propensity of the economy during 1932–7. Moreover, in chapter 5 we showed that the disaggregated evidence also assigns an important role to tariffs.

Of course such a shift in the growth performance of the economy could also be viewed as a supply side shift. In this perspective, the recovery of the 1930s is best perceived as a 'natural recovery'; the import propensity shift discussed above could also be viewed in similar terms. Before we can evaluate the role of tariffs in explaining the improved economic performance of the 1930s we need to consider the various arguments for a natural recovery.

A natural recovery?

A number of interpretations can be given to the idea of a natural recovery. First we can emphasise the 'catching up' aspects of British economic growth in the 1930s. During 1899–1929 a large technological gap arose with respect to the fast growing economies. Britain could thus borrow technology and follow existing demand patterns very easily. Thus, in this perspective the relative trend acceleration of the 1930s should be seen as a function of the initial conditions existing in the 1920s.

The method used to proxy the size of the technological gap existing in Britain in 1929 involves comparing the labour productivity level of the UK with the US level on the assumption that there exists a relationship between the productivity level and the technological level (see table 6.4).[10] Employing Maddison's productivity relatives for 1965 and extrapolating backwards we present the trends of British productivity relative to those of the US for the period 1870–1938. During 1870–1929 the British relative was falling by about 1 per cent per annum. The period 1929–38 represents a major trend reversal; for the first time in fifty years Britain started closing the size of the technological gap.

The existence of a technological gap simply defines a supply potential for the economy. There is no underlying reason as to why the gap should have started to close in 1932. The size of the gap was also substantial in 1913 and 1924 and yet aggregate growth performance between 1913–29 and 1924–9 was poor relative to the 1930s.[11] Thus in order to be able to use this idea as an aid to understanding the specific nature and timing of recovery between 1932 and 1937 we need to note that policy initiatives may have been acting on very favourable initial growth conditions. Such an analysis would emphasise strong interrelatedness between aggregate supply conditions and demand influences on economic growth.

Table 6.4 *Output per worker in 1965 US $ measured at US relative prices*
(USA = 100)

	British relative	% change per annum
1870	1.14	—
1900	0.89	−0.86
1913	0.76	−0.94
1929	0.65	−0.73
1938	0.67	+0.25

Sources: Maddison (1967, 1979, 1980).

A second natural recovery mechanism stresses the effect of the favourable terms of trade shift for the British economy during 1929–32; during this period the collapse of world primary commodity prices generated a 20.8 per cent improvement in Britain's terms of trade. Moreover, given the small size of the domestic primary producing sector and the collapse of world trade, the beneficial effects on domestic aggregate demand more than compensated for any adverse effects. Thus, consumer real wages rose rapidly between 1929 and 1932, sustaining aggregate consumption and moderating the amplitude of the depression. Another strand of this idea is that the terms of trade improvement generated a large demand for durables during the recovery as domestic incomes rose. However, from 1933 to 1937 the terms of trade deteriorated by approximately 10 per cent. Hence, most of the beneficial effects of the terms of trade served to ameliorate the depression; the explanation for the strength of revival has to be sought in other influences.

A third aspect of the natural recovery perspective has focused on the behaviour of real wages and structural shifts in the labour market (Beenstock *et al.*, 1984; Beenstock and Warburton, 1986). Within this perspective the rise of unemployment during the 1929–32 depression was partly due to the increased unwillingness to work caused by too high real benefits and partly by too high real wages, induced by *unanticipated* price falls. After 1932 this process is assumed to have gone into reverse.

It was shown in chapter 1 that it is not possible to distinguish a long-term relationship between real wages and economic growth. This conclusion is reinforced by examining the behaviour of real wages in the interwar period. Dimsdale (1984) has calculated a variety of measures for real wages for the period 1920–38. Figure 6.1 shows these measures for manufacturing and figure 6.2 for all industries. Retail real wages show a persistent upward trend from 1924 to 1935 and do not decline until 1936. Thus, this evidence

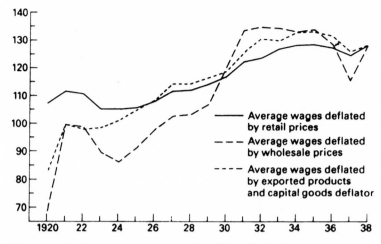

Figure 6.1 Real wages in manufacturing 1920– 1938 (1938 prices)
Source: Dimsdale (1984), table 1, p. 95.

Figure 6.2 Real wages in all industries 1920–1938 (1938 prices)
Source: Dimsdale (1984), table 2, p. 97.

does not support the contention that the behaviour of real wages changed after 1932.

In terms of the demand for labour it is necessary to consider the cost of labour to the firm and this requires an indicator of own product real wages. The absence of a suitable price deflator makes it difficult to draw any firm conclusions. One measure that has been used in the literature is to deflate wages by wholesale prices (see figures 6.1 and 6.2). These indices show a rapid increase of real wages between 1929 and 1932 before stabilising between 1932 and 1936. However, the use of the wholesale price index as a deflator is seriously flawed. The index up to 1930 reflected movements in both input and output prices and it is only the latter that is applicable to the measurement of own product real wages. The distortions caused by using this index are particularly severe in the interwar period due to the volatility of raw material prices. In an attempt to overcome this problem Dimsdale calculated own product real wages using a weighted average of export and capital goods prices as one price index and the GDP deflator as another.[12] Both these series rise throughout the recovery and peak during the mid 1930s. Thus, given the fact that the magnitude of the observed changes in own product real wages was small and the fact that any fall occurred after the recovery had started shows that the real wage argument is not supported by the data.

A final interpretation of the natural recovery approach is the view that the technological and demand structure of the 1930s generated a supply side shift with the decline of the traditional staples and the rapid growth of new industries (such as motor cars, precision instruments, dyestuffs, synthetic chemicals and consumer durables). Such industries are thought to form a self-contained 'new development block' with complementarity of demand between the different industries and strong input-output links within the new sectors. Since many of these industries were not subject to the change in commercial policy in 1932 (being already protected as new industries) the tariffs of the 1930s could not account for economic revival.

A study of these industries using the detailed industry tables of the Censuses of Production for 1924, 1930 and 1935 reveals that these 'modern' industries were indeed growing rapidly when compared to other industries. Between 1924 and 1930 output growth in these industries was significantly higher than the output growth of the other industries (see chapter 5). Between 1930 and 1935 the modern industries grew even faster. However, although these industries were growing rapidly their small share in industrial production limited their overall impact. This group of industries accounted for only 10 per cent of manufacturing output in 1924 and nearly 20 per cent in 1935. Hence, most of the acceleration of growth in the 1930s is accounted for by the established traditional industries.

A more important criticism of the new development block idea is that the input-output tables for 1930 and 1935 suggest that the backward linkages from the new industries ran predominantly back to the old staples rather than other new industries (Von Tunzelman, 1982). Hence, any policy shift that stimulated the old staple industries, such as tariffs, would have major effects on overall economic performance.

This overview of natural recovery influences suggests that many of the arguments are empirically invalid or that by themselves they are not capable of explaining all the characteristics of economic revival in the 1930s. There is no doubt that some supply conditions were favourable to growth. However, by themselves they only define a *potential*. Thus, trade policy acted to improve Britain's competitive position at a time when favourable supply conditions also existed.

Conclusion

By distinguishing the timing of recovery from the strength of recovery it is possible to clarify a number of aspects of the economic recovery in the 1930s. There is no doubt that a number of policy initiatives contributed to the turning point from depression to recovery in 1932. However, of the different policy instruments only tariffs can account for the trend improvement of the economy in the 1930s. This is not equivalent to saying that tariffs, in themselves, account for all the characteristics of economic revival in this period. An overview of the 'natural' influences on the recovery suggests that it is the *interaction* of a changed trade policy with the 'natural' influences that explain why Britain performed well in the 1930s compared to its past and to other major industrial countries. In neglecting the role of trade policy the traditional literature has neglected an important catalyst to economic revival in the period.

Conclusions

The impact of protection in the 1930s

The performance of the UK economy improved significantly in the decade of the 1930s. The evidence presented suggests that the role of tariffs in this economic revival has been underemphasised in much of the previous historical literature. Between 1932 and 1937 the UK economy witnessed a marked fall in import ratios and import propensities that could be partly attributed to the impact of the General Tariff. A comparison of import and export competitiveness shows that export competitiveness improved by 2.5 per cent in the period 1931–7 relative to 1929, while import competitiveness improved by 5.4 per cent compared to 1929 or 7.1 per cent when compared to the period 1925–31. The impact of the tariff on imports is verified by estimates of UK manufacturing import functions for the interwar years. The tariff effect is estimated to be significant and much larger than a simple relative price effect. This could either be because the tariff is capturing a long-run price elasticity of demand or because the tariff had feedback macroeconomic effects on the economy. The changes in the pattern of British import shares from different trading blocs provides further evidence of a tariff effect.

The newly protected sector of 1932 saw an improvement in economic performance relative to the poor performance of the 1920s; these industries increased their annual growth rate by 3.9 per cent in the period 1930–5 compared with 1924–30. In contrast the group of industries protected throughout the interwar saw a fairly constant growth performance between the two periods. Similar results were obtained in a study of employment, productivity, imports, exports and import propensities.

These conclusions need to be kept in perspective. Tariffs were successful in stimulating economic revival, partly bcause they were acting as a catalyst in the context of very favourable conditions. For example, devaluation contributed to the recovery by improving competitiveness and facilitating the introduction of cheap money in 1932. Similarly there were no binding constraints that prevented policy from being effective. In particular, the process of wage bargaining did not prevent the new trade policies from generating improved competitiveness and initiating import substitution.

Care must be taken when drawing policy implications from this study. The evidence we have evaluated has been considered from the perspective of analysing the historical experience of the UK in the 1930s – we are not offering a general theory of protectionism. Thus, our conclusion that tariffs were important to the recovery of the 1930s does not imply that they generated an industrial structure that was beneficial to economic growth after the Second World War. To the extent that tariffs gave a new life to the old staple sectors, they may have actually prevented the necessary structural change that would have accelerated long-term economic growth in the 1950–73 boom.

Moreover, it does not necessarily follow from our results that a general tariff should have been introduced much earlier. The case for imposing tariffs in the 1870s, when the rest of the world was moving to a long phase of tariff protection, needs to be considered in its own right with a detailed study of British relative economic decline between 1873 and 1913. However, by the interwar years the level of tariffs in the world economy was very high and, in the light of an exchange rate policy that over-priced British goods in the 1920s, a general tariff in 1920–1, say, would most probably have benefitted the UK economy through similar processes to those we have discussed for the 1930s.

Implications for trade policy in contemporary Britain

The experience of interwar Britain has often been used for drawing homologies with current economic problems. In considering trade policy, however, a primary concern must be the different economic conditions prevailing in the two periods. The potential of trade policy being used to alter competitiveness and trade flows is significantly lower today than it was in the interwar period. The exchange rate is substantially determined by capital movements and domestic monetary policy, preventing exchange rate management from acting concertedly on merchandise trade. Furthermore, the institutions of price and wage setting limit the potential for trade policy to alter relative prices. Increases in the costs of food and raw materials are rapidly passed on to final prices and real wage resistance leads to increases in money wages and unit labour costs.

Even if it was possible to generate a policy induced improvement in competitiveness it is questionable whether this would lead to import substitution and the expansion of exports. Non-price factors, such as quality and speed of delivery, are increasingly important in determining trade flows; an exchange rate or a protectionist policy would not directly affect these non-price influences. Secondly, favourable output effects are dependent on the existence of sufficient excess capacity. Although there currently exists substantial unemployment the structure of production and trade requires the increasing use of specific inputs. Thus the existence of an excess supply of labour is not sufficient to facilitate economic growth; what is required is a supply of labour with the required skills. In interwar Britain much of the recovery took place in traditional industries which utilised existing skills.

One of the features of a protectionist policy is that it can be directed at competitive imports without raising the prices of complementary imports. Thus the tariff of 1932 was not applied to raw materials. It has however become increasingly difficult to identify competitive imports. The international structure of production has become far more complex. The division of the production process across national boundaries by multinational corporations has made it difficult to distinguish between inputs and finished products. Moreover, specialisation and technical sophistication has reduced the potential for import substitution.

One of the deciding factors in favour of protectionism in 1931/2 was the use of discriminatory trade policies by other trading nations. Britain, which had remained essentially free trade, had been progressively squeezed out of overseas markets by the protectionist measures of its competitors. This substantially limited the scope for effective retaliation in response to the General Tariff. Conversely current trading relations are conducted within a broadly free trade system. Thus an independently pursued protectionist policy would be severely threatened by retaliation.

The impact of tariffs in interwar Britain indicates that universal adherence to the doctrine of free trade may not always be appropriate to an industrialised economy in disequilibrium. As such, our results are consistent with much of recent trade theory literature which stresses a positive role for protection under conditions of oligopoly and imperfect competition (Venables and Smith, 1986; Brander and Spencer, 1983 and 1985; Krugman, 1987). In the context of current policy formulation our research suggests that the approach to trade policy should be more flexible than is allowed for in a free trade paradigm. Policy instruments should be constructed in the context of prevailing economic conditions and not solely with reference to restrictive theoretical perspectives.

Notes

Introduction

1 Quoted in N. Kaldor (1977), 'The Nemesis of Free Trade', *Further Essays on Applied Economics*, p. 236.
2 A total of 6,500 items were listed under the Safeguarding of Industries Act but the total value of goods affected was very low. The duties were *ad valorem* at a rate of $33\frac{1}{3}$ per cent.
3 There were many critics of Keynes' proposals, such as Robbins, who argued that a tariff would induce compensating money wage demands which would leave profits and employment unchanged.
4 Opponents of a tariff responded by arguing that a fall in import demand would depress foreign income and the demand for Britain's exports.
5 The size of an economy will also be relevant in that it may influence the magnitude of retaliation from trading partners.

1 British interwar economic growth in an historical perspective

1 Maddison's approach sees each epoch as historically unique. His perspective contrasts with the Kondratieff wave literature which explains each 'epoch' as part of a long cyclical process. However, we regard Maddison's framework as more relevant to understanding the path of the British economy since Kondratieff long waves have not been observed in British long-run historical data (Solomou, 1987).
2 The compromise estimate is derived as an average of the income, expenditure and output estimates of GDP. In addition Feinstein (1972) has used the adjusted expenditure estimate, which includes some revisions to make the cyclical path in the series more comparable to that of the income estimate.

3 Feinstein (1972) suggested the following reliabilities to the components of GDP:

	1870–1890		1891–1913	
	Value	Volume	Value	Volume
Consumption	C	C	B	B
Investment	C/D	D	C	C
Government consumption	B	C	B	C
Exports	B	B	B	B
Imports	B	B	B	B
Factor cost adjustment	B	C	A	A/B
GDP (output)	C	C	B	B
GDP (income)	C	–	B	–

He indicates that the following errors are associated with each letter:

$A = \pm \leqslant 5\%$
$B = \pm 5\%$ to 15%
$C = \pm 15\%$ to 25%
$D = \pm > 25\%$

4 By a 'trend period' the historical growth literature means a phase of economic growth; the long-wave literature uses the term to describe the growth behaviour of the economy during half a cycle.

5 The Central Statistical Office of the UK will be applying a similar technique to provide 'balanced' GDP estimates for the more recent periods.

6 The reliability values were taken by those assigned by Feinstein (1972). For a detailed breakdown see Solomou and Weale (1988).

7 A 'long swing' is used here in terms of the Kuznets swing literature to capture a swing of approximately eighteen to thirty years periodicity.

8 This conclusion is also verified if we examine the growth trends of the income and expenditure series of GDP individually, rather than as an average in the compromise estimate. Both series show the Edwardian period as being a downswing in economic growth but not a climacteric. In these terms the best explanations of the Edwardian climacteric is that it is a statistical artefact (Solomou, 1987; Greasley, 1986).

9 Of course the period 1929–37 represents both a relative trend revival of the economy *and* a major cyclical recovery between 1932 and 1937. A complete explanation of economic revival in the 1930s needs to consider both phenomena.

10 For an outline of the statistical methodology see Solomou, 1987, chapter 2.

11 These real wage indices will be important in different ways. The consumer real wage will influence the supply of labour as it affects the choice between leisure and work; producer real wages will influence the demand for labour; and tradable product wages will capture international competitive influences facing the UK labour market. See chapter 6 for a further discussion of real wages.

2 The impact of protectionism on economic growth: theoretical issues

1 The optimum tariff may not be beneficial to A if retaliation occurs. If the response of B to A's protection is to retaliate the end position may leave A and B both worse off than under free trade. We do not take up the important issue of retaliation here for a number of reasons. First, the difficult analytical problems that arise would require a more extensive study of the structure of the interwar world economy. Secondly, the evidence for extensive retaliation against Britain in 1932 is extremely weak (Eichengreen, 1981b). Britain and the Netherlands were the only two countries to follow a free trade regime in a protectionist world economy. Moreover, even in 1932 the average level of the British tariff was still lower than other countries (Friedman, 1974, table 23). Finally, if successful retaliation against Britain was observed we should observe a greater fall in British exports relative to the fall observed for the world economy. In fact the British export fall was comparable to the world average (see chapter 5).

2 Such results are not universal. Krishna (1983) considers a duopoly model where the home and foreign firm are unable to sustain collusion under free trade. However, if the domestic government imposes an import quota this may facilitate collusion. The quota restricts price competition from the foreign firm, allowing the home firm to raise its price. This, in turn, allows the foreign firm to sell its quota amount at a higher price. The domestic consumers end up being the losers.

3 In this specification consumption and, thus, savings are seen to be determined by current income.

4 Using a simple income-expenditure model Harrod (1933) showed that:

$$Y = \frac{1}{m} X$$

where

Y = real income
X = real exports
m = marginal propensity to import

Kennedy and Thirwell (1979) show how this can be extended in a more complicated income-expenditure model.

3 Quantitative studies of the impact of the 1932 General Tariff

1 That is the advantage accruing to individual domestic industries from the imposition of an import tariff on competing goods.

2 A more general summary of various qualitative views on the impact of the 1932 tariff can be found in Capie (1983, pp. 96–106).

3 The limitations of using 1930 as a base year are discussed by Leak (1937, pp. 568 and 606) and Glenday (1937, p. 601).

4 Moreover, the data in table 3.1 are complicated by the compositional change in imports.

5 The group includes certain non-ferrous metals, calcium carbide, potassium compounds, finished dyestuffs, natural essential oils and newsprint.

6 This approach is limited by data problems, particularly as imported goods may
   have been qualitatively different from those goods produced domestically but in
   the same classification.
7 For the imports included in table 3.3 an average duty of 18.2 per cent was
   calculated for both 1933 and 1934.
8 It should be noted that some classes of goods were in both samples A and B.
9 The volume of production of sample B products expanded by 32 and 47 per cent
   for 1933 and 1934 compared with 1930.
10 This period, chosen because the Census of Production were taken in these years,
   is obviously not ideal as the tariff was introduced in 1931/2 and its full impact
   would take time to work through.
11 It should be noted that Richardson's figures are in *value* terms. Thus, we cannot
   compare the physical output performance of these industries from table 3.4.
12 For the concept to be operational would require rational expectations and
   perfect capital mobility, assumptions which do not seem valid for the 1930s.
13 Foreman-Peck's treatment of exchange rate changes in this period is inadequate.
   Although the £–$ rate was fairly constant between 1930 and 1935, there existed
   significant variations in the real effective exchange rate (see chapter 4).
   Moreover, Foreman-Peck ignores the possibility that tariffs may actually *cause*
   an appreciation of the exchange rate in a flexible exchange rate regime (see
   chapter 2).
14 Foreman-Peck (1981) gives an estimate of 2.3 per cent for the increase in GNP.
   This is due to a calculation error on his part as he has manufacturing imports
   falling with an increase in domestic income instead of rising. The change in
   income due to the tariff can be calculated as

   = multiplier × share of manufactured imports in national income × change in
     imports due to the tariff
   = 1.75 × 0.056 × 0.41 = 0.041

15 Broadberry (1986, p. 135) notes on Eichengreen's (1979) empirical results: 'The
   control simulations are very poor, and one need not be too surprised at the
   peculiar results implied by the counterfactual simulations.'

4 A macroeconomic analysis of the impact of the 1932 General Tariff

1 The fall in import propensities was observed in most industries, the largest
   reductions being experienced in the vehicle industry, textiles, iron and steel,
   clothing, electrical goods and chemicals (see chapter 5). Only in the raw material
   based industries of timber and paper did any significant fall fail to occur. Such
   a disaggregated picture suggests that import propensity changes were observed
   both in the newly protected sectors of 1931/2 and the industries that were
   already protected. Hence, the tariff cannot be seen as the only influence on
   sectoral import propensity changes.
2 Although some protection was afforded to the domestic agricultural sector, in
   that a tariff was imposed on food imports from non-British countries, its scope

was limited by Imperial Preference and by the fact that most of British trade in agricultural products was conducted in the sterling bloc.

3 During 1924–9 constant (1938) price food imports increased by 1.4 per cent per annum while during 1929–37 they fell by 1.26 per cent per annum.

4 To the extent that tariffs and other policies stimulated aggregate growth, the food import ratio would be expected to fall as income rose.

5 The average exchange rate of Dimsdale (1981) used each country's share in world trade as weights while the manufacturing exchange rate is constructed using shares in UK overseas trade. There are also small differences in the countries covered. The sterling effective exchange rate shown in table 4.3 (column 2) was constructed by Redmond (1980) using shares in bilateral and multilateral trade as weights. It indicates an average sterling devaluation of approximately 5 per cent in the period 1932–7 compared with the 1929–30 level. The average exchange rate (column 3) and the manufacturing exchange rate (column 4) show a greater devaluation, 22.6 per cent and 14.4 per cent respectively, compared with 1929. As both these indicators are based on manufacturing trade they are influenced by the European gold bloc currencies which were comparatively over-valued against sterling. Thus they indicate a higher devaluation for manufacturing trade as opposed to the effective rate which is influenced by the currencies of raw material and food exporters. A striking point is the difference between the average exchange rate and the manufacturing rate. In part this can be explained by coverage and alternative weighting procedures. The major divergence however arises after 1933 and is primarily due to our decision to adjust for a 35 per cent devaluation of the German exchange rate for the period 1933–8. Germany operated a complex multiple exchange rate regime during this period with an effective devaluation of the official rate for trade in manufactures (Kindleberger, 1956, p.116).

6 Leak (1937) calculated average rates of duty of 17.2 per cent for 1932, 18.5 per cent for 1933, 19.4 per cent for 1934, declining to 19.3 per cent in 1935. This is higher than our figure of 13.2 per cent because we have included in our calculations those imports of manufactures not subject to the policy change in 1932 (see appendix 4.1).

7 Of course the extent of the tariff did mean that it raised the prices of some inputs, most notably iron and steel.

8 The tariff indicators used in estimating the regressions reported in tables 4.5 and 4.6 were those of Leak and the manufacturing tariff rate calculated in appendix 4.1. We also estimated the equations using the average revenue tariff. The latter is simply calculated as total customs receipts as a percentage of total imports. Since we are estimating manufacturing import functions the latter is not really appropriate. However, similar significant results are obtained.

9 Scott (1963) estimated a tariff elasticity of six. Our estimates are comparable to those of Morgan and Martin (1975) for the postwar period.

10 If we constrain the coefficient of the tariff variable to equal that of the relative price variable by estimating:

$$\ln M = a + b \ln Y + c \ln P(1 + \tau) + \varepsilon_t$$

the fit of this equation is significantly worse with an R^2 value of only 0.29. Clearly, the tariff may be reducing imports by changing the competitiveness of the domestic economy via various feedback mechanisms. If the tariff generates investment and, thus, economies of scale, we could expect a non-linear relationship between tariffs and imports. Morgan and Martin (1975) also note that the tariff elasticity may be significantly higher than the price elasticity because of the imposition of prohibitive or near-prohibitive import duties.

11 In looking at shares we are overcoming some of the problems of using current price data, especially since the level of disaggregation we are employing involves calculating shares for comparable commodities.

12 The main trading nations in this group were Australia, New Zealand, Canada, India, Ceylon and South Africa.

13 The gold bloc consists of Belgium, France, Netherlands, Switzerland, Italy and Poland.

14 These treaties were signed between 1933 and 1935 by Argentina, Denmark, Norway, Sweden, Finland and Poland.

15 The major trading countries in this group were Spain, Czechoslovakia, China, Japan, Egypt, Brazil, Uruguay and Russia.

16 This proposition requires that the price and income elasticities are similar for the different blocs. Thus, food exports from the gold bloc are implicitly assumed to be the same commodity as for the other zones.

17 See appendix 5.1 for a detailed outline of the newly protected industries in 1932.

18 Given that the trend estimates are simply used to *describe* the data we have assumed a one-tailed 95 per cent confidence test on the significance of the trend coefficient. Where the t-test is not significant we have assumed that the coefficient for the trend is equal to zero in the inter-period trend comparisons.

19 This is the implication of Glickman's study of Imperial Preference (Glickman, 1947).

20 Thus, although Capie (1983) is correct to emphasise the rising trend in the share of imports from British countries between 1870–1937, the rapidly increasing trend of the 1930s needs to be emphasised, particularly in the light of fairly constant levels in the 1920s.

21 Table 4.8 shows that during 1931–7 the decline of the share of the gold bloc countries was greater than the core competitors. However, it would be misleading only to look at the 1930s since the underlying trends of the 1920s were so different.

22 As can be seen from figure 4.6 the share of the core competitors began falling from 1930. Our discussion does not aim to explain all the observed fluctuations; however, given that a higher proportion of imports from core competitors consisted of high income elastic products, these would be the first to decline in a depression.

23 The share of the largest countries in this residual category (Spain, Czechoslovakia, China, Japan, Egypt, Brazil, Uruguay, Russia) remained constant throughout 1924–37, suggesting that it was the small countries that gained most in the 1930s.

24 Many of these economies were performing well in the recovery of the 1930s.

25 Countries like Japan and Brazil were undergoing a period of trend accelerated economic growth from the 1930s.

5 Industrial performance and trade policy: a disaggregated analysis

1 We use the phrase 'non-newly protected' to denote either those industries that were already protected under earlier legislation or those industries that were not protected.

2 At this level of disaggregation much of the data are measured in value rather than volume.

3 This is, of course, a simplification. Some imports will be used as an input in export industries. As world exports stagnated in the 1930s this would have repercussion effects on imports.

4 Since vehicles represent an outlier in import propensity behaviour and the production data do not exist for the pre-1920 period we have excluded the industry from the regression estimation.

5 As the Harrod multiplier is not expected to hold for any one industry individually we also estimated the simple relationship:

$$\Delta g_{Qi} = \alpha \Delta m_i$$

This should pick up the significance of a sectoral import substitution process; if $\hat{\alpha}$ is negative and significant this can be taken as *prima facie* evidence for an import substitution process. For the period 1900–37 we estimated the following equation using the data for the first ten industries in table 5.2 (t-values in parenthesis):

$$\Delta g_{Qi} = -0.50536 \Delta m_i$$
$$(6.54)$$

Similar results were obtained for the period 1913–37

$$\Delta g_{Qi} = -0.56975 \Delta m_i$$
$$-(5.39)$$

6 The Census of Production data was also supplemented by information from the Annual Statement of Trade. In order to make the trade data comparable to the production data we reclassified exports and retained imports accordingly.

7 As pointed out in chapter 3 a comparison of relative performance for the period 1930–5 would only be relevant if the sectoral growth paths in the 1920s were on a steady and balanced growth path.

8 The food, drink and tobacco industry has been excluded from the comparison of newly protected with non-newly protected industries. The protection of this group of industries was covered by various legislation (including revenue duties) throughout the period. Thus, there was not a single policy shift following the introduction of the General Tariff in 1931/2. Furthermore many competing imports benefited from Imperial Preference.

9 The data in table 5.3 are in current price terms; meaningful volume data are not

possible to calculate because appropriate deflators are not available. However, since our interest is in relative sectoral performance this would only be a serious problem if there were *major* sectoral relative price shifts during 1924–30 and 1930–5.

10 These data can be compared with those of Richardson (1967, table 20), who for the period 1930–5 shows that the imports of the newly protected group fell by 7.8 per cent per annum while the non-newly protected group fell by 8.8 per cent per annum. The discrepancies between these numbers and those of table 5.3 are due to the errors that result from defining industrial groups from data sources that do not correspond one for one. However, we have attempted to limit this problem by using a finer level of industrial disaggregation than Richardson.

11 It should be noted that world trade in manufactures fell by 4.2 per cent per annum during the period.

12 Import penetration for industry is defined here as:

$$\frac{P_m M}{P_n N - P_x X + P_m M}$$

where

M = import volume whose price is P_m

X = export volume whose price is P_x

N = Volume of domestic output, whose price is P_n

This measure differs from that reported in table 1.10 in a number of respects. First, the figures in table 5.4 are a value measure, therefore they reflect changes in both volume and prices. Secondly, in table 1.10 the measure for total manufacturing gross output includes the food, drink and tobacco industry whereas trade in this activity was classified elsewhere. Thus if food, drink and tobacco is excluded, as in table 5.4, it will raise the import penetration figures. Lastly, the figures in table 5.4 use gross output figures from the Censuses of Production which exclude firms that have less than ten employees (although the 1924 Census did cover such small firms the figures used here are the adjusted totals which allow comparison with 1930 and 1935). As the Census based figures will be lower than the true figure it will also tend to raise the import penetration levels. The figures are, thus, more interesting in terms of rates of change rather than levels.

13 These growth rates are, of course, dependent on the weights used and the method of calculation. The results reported here are calculated as:

$$g_t = \frac{\sum_{i=1}^{n} X_{it} W_i}{\sum_{i=1}^{n} X_{it-1} W_i}$$

where X_i = volume of production in industry i:

W_i = weight of industry i measured as net output in 1930 as a proportion of total output in 1930

A logarithmic approximation to this equation yields slightly different numbers (see statistical appendix 5.2) but these do not affect the nature of the argument. It should be noted that the volume of production index is based on the principal products of the trade whereas the net output figure is based on the total output of the trade. For most industries there are only small differences in the two sets of figures.

14 As can be seen from the statistical appendix these statements are validated using formal statistical testing. Using a t-test on the differences in the mean growth path of two samples shows that the already protected sectors grew on a steady path between the period 1924–30 and 1930–5 ($t = 0.4$) while the newly protected sector saw a significant increase in output growth ($t = 3.17$). The significance tests also show that the initial growth performance of the two sectors differed significantly between 1924 and 1930 ($t = 2.48$) but was not statistically significant between 1930 and 1935 ($t = 0.81$). Thus, if we apply Richardson's perspective and focus on the period 1930–5 we cannot distinguish a significant difference in the performance of newly protected and the already protected sectors. However, the inter-period significance tests show how totally misleading this result is.

15 As the employment figures are taken from the Census of Production they differ from other estimates such as those reported in Feinstein (1972) which make adjustments for self-employed and part-time employees.

16 It will be apparent that the boundaries between the different categories are not clear cut and that competitiveness in many industries will depend on a mix of characteristics. Allowing for this caveat we feel that the approach is useful in capturing the dominant characteristic of an industry.

17 The food; drink and tobacco industries have been included in the non-newly protected group of resource based activities.

18 Since the calculation of effective protection rates is complicated and subject to errors, our reservations may relate more to the calculated effective protection rates than the validity of the concept.

6 The 1930s economic revival: an overview

1 Most studies of economic recovery in the 1930s have focused exclusively on the issue of the turning point, neglecting relative trend improvement.

2 The Marshall-Lerner condition is satisfied when the absolute sum of the import and export price elasticities sum to one or above. During the interwar period Broadberry (1986) estimates that the price elasticities of demand for exports and imports were -1.5 and -0.5 respectively. In calculating the improvement in the balance of trade he assumes that the favourable conditions for exporters lead to an increase in mark-ups while the adverse conditions for importers resulted in a fall in the mark-up. Thus, a 13 per cent depreciation is assumed to lead to a fall in the foreign price of British exports of 8 per cent and a rise in the sterling price of imports of 9 per cent.

3 More than two dozen countries allowed their currencies to depreciate with sterling, including the Empire countries, Scandinavia, Eastern Europe, Portugal, Argentina and Egypt.

4 Devaluation may have also generated some 'price surprise', inflating the domestic price level and reducing real wages which, in turn, generated supply side responses in the labour market.

5 Changes in the structure of company finance during the interwar period reduced the importance of external finance from banks and the capital market.

6 One third of bank advances in the 1930s went to individuals.

7 This fact is important in the light of Capie's (1983) comment that the effective protection rates suggest a hindrance to a leading sector such as building. The national accounting data suggest that manufacturing was the leading sector.

8 An alternative measure is provided by the concept of fiscal leverage. This begins with the idea that the multiplier effect of different components of fiscal measures is variable. Hence, in any specific period a weighting structure is needed to calculate the impact of fiscal policy. Using this concept, and allowing for price level effects Broadberry (1984) has calculated that fiscal policy was broadly neutral during 1930–4. However, the Pigou price level effects Broadberry analyses provide an incomplete analysis of price effects in a depression period such as 1929–32 (Solomou, 1987, pp. 72–3).

9 Thomas (1983) has estimated that during 1935–8 both the direct and indirect labour needs of rearmament created one million jobs.

10 Of course we do not really know what specific form this relationship took in the 1930s. A simple linear assumption would be unrealistic.

11 While British GDP growth averaged one third the world average during 1913–29 this increased to twice the world average between 1929 and 1937.

12 Dimsdale has also calculated a series for product real wages in the whole economy using the final expenditure deflator. As import prices are included in the deflator this series exhibits slightly different behaviour to the series using the GDP deflator. In particular the increase during the depression is greater and the increase during the recovery lower. The series however also peaks in 1936.

References

The following abbreviations are used in the list of references:

E.E.H.   *Explorations in Economic History*
Ec.H.R.   *Economic History Review*
E.J.   *Economic Journal*
J.E.H.   *Journal of Economic History*
J.P.E.   *Journal of Political Economy*
O.E.P.   *Oxford Economic Papers*
J.R.S.S.   *Journal of the Royal Statistical Society*

Aldcroft, D.H. (1967): 'Economic growth in Britain in the interwar years: a reassessment', *Ec.H.R.*, 20: 311–26.
  (1974): 'McCloskey on Victorian growth: a comment', *Ec.H.R.*, 27: 271–4.
  (1986a): *The British Economy*, vol. 1, Wheatsheaf, Brighton.
  (1986b): 'Great Britain – the constraints to full employment in the 1930s and 1980s, in I. Berend, and K. Boorchardt (eds.), *The Impact of the Depression in the 1930s and Its Relevance for the Contemporary World*, Karl Marx University of Economics, Budapest.
Aldcroft, D.H. and Fearon, P. (eds.) (1969): *Economic Growth in 20th Century Britain*, Macmillan, London.
Alford, B.W.E. (1972): *Depression and Recovery? British Economic Growth, 1918–1939*, Macmillan, London.
Arndt, H.W. (1944): *The Economic Lessons of the 1930s*, Oxford University Press for the Royal Institute of International Affairs, Oxford.
Bairoch, P. (1976): 'Europe's Gross National Product: 1800–1975', *Journal of European Economics History*, 5: 273–340.
  (1986): 'Commercial policies and economic development in history: myth and reality of protectionism', *Journal of Regional Policy*, 4, 86: 512–34.
Bank of England (1984): 'The UK economic recovery in the 930s', Panel Paper 23, April.
Barna, T. (1952): 'The interdependence of the British economy', *J.R.S.S.*, series A: 29–77.
Beenstock, M., Capie, F. and Griffiths, B. (1984): 'Economic recovery in the UK' in the Bank of England Panel Paper, 23, April: 57–85.
Beenstock, M. and Warburton, P. (1983): 'Long term trends in economic openness in the United Kingdom and the United States', *O.E.P.*, 35: 130–40.
  (1986): 'Wages and unemployment in interwar Britain', *E.E.H.*, 23: 153–72.

Benjamin, D.K. and Kochin, L.A. (1979a): 'Searching for an explanation of unemployment in interwar Britain', *J.P.E.*, 87: 441–70.

(1979b): 'What went right with juvenile unemployment policy between the wars: a comment', *Ec.H.R.*, 32: 523–8.

Benjamin, D.K., Kochin, L.A., Collins, M., Cross, R., Metcalf, D., Nickell, S.J., Floros, N., Ormerod, P.A. and Worswick, G.D.N. (1982): 'Symposium on unemployment in interwar Britain', *J.P.E.*, 90.

Birkett (1937): 'Reply to Leak', *J.R.S.S.*, 100: 597–602.

Board of Trade (annual): *Journal*, HMSO, London.

Booth, A. and Glynn, S. (1975): 'Unemployment in the interwar period: a multiple problem', *Journal of Contemporary History*, 10: 611–36.

Boyer, R. (1977): 'Commercial policy under alternative exchange rate regimes', *Canadian Journal of Economics*, 10: 218–32.

Brander, J.A. and Spencer, B.J. (1981): 'Tariffs and the extraction of foreign monopoly rents under potential entry', *Canadian Journal of Economics*, 14: 371–89.

(1983): 'International R & D rivalry and industrial strategy', *Review of Economic Studies*, 50: 707–22.

(1984): 'Tariff protection and imperfect competition', in H. Kierzhkowski (ed.), *Monopolistic Competition in International Trade*, Oxford University Press.

(1985): 'Export subsidies and international market share rivalry', *Journal of International Economics*, 18: 83–100.

Broadberry, S.N. (1983): 'Unemployment in interwar Britain: a disequilibrium approach', *O.E.P.*, 35: 463–85.

(1986): *The British Economy Between the Wars: A Macroeconomic Survey*, Basil Blackwell, Oxford.

BSO (1978): *Historical Record of the Census of Production, 1907–70*.

Buxton, N.K. (1975): 'The role of the "new industries" in Britain during the 1930s: a reinterpretation', *Business History Review*, 49: 205–22.

Cairncross, A.K. and Eichengreen, B.J. (1983): *Sterling in Decline*, Basil Blackwell, Oxford.

Capie, F. (1978): 'The British Tariff and industrial protection in the 1930s', *Ec.H.R.*, 31: 399–409.

(1980): 'The pressure for tariff protection in Britain, 1917–31', *Journal of European Economic History*, 2: 431–48.

(1981): 'Tariffs, elasticities and prices in Britain in the 1930s', *Ec.H.R.*, 34: 140–2.

(1983): *Depression and Protectionism: Britain Between the Wars*, George Allen & Unwin, London.

Capie, F. and Collins, M. (1980): 'The extent of British recovery in the 1930s', *Economy and History*, 23: 40–60.

(1983): *The Interwar Economy: A Statistical Abstract*, Manchester University Press, Manchester.

Casson, M. (1983): *Economics of Unemployment: An Historical Perspective*, Martin Robinson, Oxford.

Chan, K. (1978): 'The employment effects of tariffs under a free exchange rate regime', *Journal of International Economics*, 8: 415–24.

Corden, W.M. (1967): 'Australian tariff policy', *Australian Economic Papers*, 6: 131–54.

(1971): *The Theory of Protection*, Clarendon Press, Oxford.

Corner, D.C. (1956): 'Exports and the British trade cycle: 1929', *The Manchester School*, 24: 124–60.

Crafts, N.F.R. (1979): 'Victorian Britain did fail', *Ec.H.R.*, 32: 533–7.

(1984): 'Economic growth in France and Britain, 1830–1910: a review of the evidence', *J.E.H.*, 44: 49–67.

(1985): *British Economic Growth During the Industrial Revolution*, Oxford University Press.

(1987): 'Long term unemployment in Britain in the 1930s', *Ec.H.R.*, 40: 418–32.

Crafts, N.F.R. and Thomas, M. (1986): 'Comparative advantage in U.K. manufacturing trade, 1910–1935', *E.J.*, 96: 629–45.

Crafts, N.F.R., Leybourne, S.J. and Mills, T.C. (1989): 'The climacteric in late Victorian Britain and France: a reappraisal of the evidence', *Journal of Applied Econometrics*, 4: 103–7.

Cripps, F. and Godley, W. (1976): 'A formal analysis of the Cambridge economic policy group model', *Economica*, 43: 335–48.

(1978): 'Control of imports as a means to full employment and the expansion of world trade: the UK's case', *Cambridge Journal of Economics*, 2: 327–34.

Customs and Excise Department (annual): *Annual Statement of the Trade of the United Kingdom with Foreign Countries and British Countries*, HMSO, London.

Dimsdale, N.H. (1981): 'British monetary policy and the exchange rate 1920–38', in W.A. Eltis and P.J.N. Sinclair (eds.), *The Money Supply and the Exchange Rate*, Oxford University Press.

(1984): 'Employment and real wages in the interwar period', *National Institute Economic Review*, 110: 94–103.

Dixit, A. (1984): 'International trade policy for oligopolistic industries', *E.J.*, 94, Supplement: 1–16.

Dornbusch, R. (1976): 'Expectations and exchange rate dynamics', *J.P.E.*, 84: 1161–76.

(1980): *Open Economy Macroeconomics*, Basic Books, New York.

Dowie, J.R. (1968): 'Growth in the interwar period: some more arithmetic', *Ec.H.R.*, 21: 93–112.

Dowie, J.A (1975): '1919–20 is in need of attention', *Ec.H.R.*, 28: 429–50.

Drummond, I.M. (1981): *The Floating Pound and the Sterling Area, 1931–1939*, Cambridge University Press.

Durand, M and Giorno, C. (1987): 'Indicators of international competitiveness: conceptual aspects and evaluation', *OECD Economic Studies*, 9, Autumn: 147–82.

Eichengreen, B.J. (1979): 'Tariffs and flexible exchange rates', Unpublished Ph.D. Dissertation, Yale University.

(1981a): 'A dynamic model of tariffs, output and employment under flexible exchange rates', *Journal of International Economics*, 11: 341–59.

(1981b): 'Sterling and the tariff, 1929–32', *Princeton Studies in International Finance*, 48.

(1987): 'Unemployment in interwar Britain: dole or doldrums?', *O.E.P.*, 39: 597–623.

Eichengreen, B. and Hatton, T.J. (eds.) (1988): *Interwar Unemployment in International Perspective*, Kluwer Academic Publishers, Dordrecht.

Eichengreen, B. and Sach, J. (1985): 'Exchange rates and economic policy in the 1930s', *J.E.H.*, 45: 925–46.

Feinstein, C.H. (1972): *National Income, Expenditure and Output of the United Kingdom, 1855–1965*, Cambridge University Press.

Feinstein, C.H., Matthews, R.C.O. and Odling-Smee, J. (1983): 'The timing of the climacteric and its sectoral incidence in the UK 1873–1913', in C.P. Kindleberger and G. di Tella (eds.), *Economics in the Long View*, Macmillan, London.

Ford, J.L. and Sen, S. (1985): *Protectionism, Exchange Rates and the Macroeconomy*, Basil Blackwell, Oxford.

Foreman-Peck, J.S. (1979): 'Tariff protection and economies of scale: the British motor car industry before 1939', *O.E.P.*, 31: 237–57.

(1981): 'The British tariff and industrial protection in the 1930s: an alternative model', *Ec.H.R.*, 34: 132–9.

Friedman, P. (1974): *The Impact of Trade Destruction on National Incomes: A Study of Europe 1924–38*, University of Florida.

(1978): 'An econometric model of national income, commercial policy and the level of international trade: the open economies of Europe, 1924–1938', *J.E.H.*, 38: 148–80.

Garside, W.R. (1977): 'Juvenile unemployment and public policy between the wars', *Ec.H.R.*, 30: 322–39.

Garside, W.R. and Hatton, T.J. (1985): 'Keynesian policy and British unemployment in the 1930s', *Ec.H.R.*, 38: 83–8.

Glenday (1937): 'Reply to Leak', *J.R.S.S.*, 100: 600–1.

Glickman, D.L. (1947): 'The British Imperial Preference System', *Quarterly Journal of Economics*, 61: 439–70.

Glynn, S. and Booth, A. (1983): 'Unemployment in interwar Britain: a case for re-learning the lessons of the 1930s', *Ec.H.R.*, 36: 329–48.

Grassman, S. (1980): 'Long-term trends in openness of national economies', *O.E.P.*, 32: 123–33.

Greasley, D. (1986): 'The paradox of the 1880s and the timing of the climacteric', *E.E.H.*, 23: 416–33.

Gylfason, T. and Helliwell, J.F. (1983): 'A synthesis of Keynesian, monetary and portfolio approaches to flexible exchange rates', *E.J.*, 93: 820–31.

Harrod, R. (1933): *International Economics*, Cambridge University Press.

Hart, P.E. (1968): *Studies in Profit, Business Saving and Investment in the UK 1920–1962*, 2 volumes, George Allen & Unwin, London.

Hatton, T.J. (1983): 'Unemployment benefits and the macroeconomics of the inter-war labour market', *O.E.P.*, 35: 486–505.

(1984): 'Vacancies and unemployment in the 1920s', Centre for Economic Policy Research Discussion Paper 10.

(1985): 'The British labor market in the 1920s: a test of the search-turnover approach', *E.E.H*, 22: 257–70.

(1986): 'Female labour force participation: the enigma of the inter-war period', Centre for Economic Policy Research Discussion Paper 113.

Heim, C.E. (1983): 'Industrial organisation and regional development in interwar Britain', *J.E.H.*, 43: 931–52.

(1984): 'Limits to intervention: the Bank of England and industrial diversification in the depressed areas', *Ec.H.R.*, 37: 533–50.

HMSO (1930–2): *Census of Production, 1924*, London.

(1933–5): *Census of Production, 1930*, London.

(1938–44): *Census of Production, 1935*, London.

Hoffman, W.G. (1955): *British Industry, 1700–1950*, Basil Blackwell, Oxford.

Houthakker, H.S. and Magee, S.P. (1969): 'Income and price elasticities in world trade', *Review of Economics and Statistics*, 60: 111–25.

Howson, S. (1974): 'The origins of dear money, 1919–20', *Ec.H.R.*, 27: 88–107.

(1975): *Domestic Monetary Management in Britain 1919–38*, Cambridge University Press.

(1981): 'Slump and unemployment' in R. Floud and D.N. McCloskey (eds.), *An Economic History of Britain since 1700*, Vol. II., Cambridge University Press.

Hughes, J.J. and Thirwall, A.P. (1977): 'Trends and cycles in import penetration in the United Kingdom', *Oxford Bulletin of Economics and Statistics*, 39: 301–17.

Humphries, J. (1987): 'Inter-war house building, cheap money and building societies: the housing boom revisited', *Business History*, 29: 325–45.

Jones, M.E.F. (1985): 'The regional impact of an overvalued pound in the 1920s', *Ec.H.R.*, 38: 393–401.

Kahn, A.E. (1946): *Great Britain in the World Economy*, Sir Isaac Pitman, London.

Kaldor, N. (1951): 'Employment policies and the problem of international balance', *Review of Economic Studies*, 19: 42–9.

(1970): 'The case for regional policies', *Scottish Journal of Political Economy*, 17: 337–48.

(1971): 'Conflicts in national economic objectives', *E.J.*, 81: 1–16.

(1977): 'The Nemesis of free trade' in N. Kaldor, *Further Essays on Applied Economics*, Duckworth, London.

(1982): 'Limitations of the "General Theory"', *Proceedings of the British Academy*, 68.

Kaldor, N. and Kitson, M. (1986): 'The impact of import restrictions in the interwar period', Report to the ESRC, Department of Applied Economics, Cambridge.

Kennedy, C. and Thirlwall, A.P. (1979): 'Import penetration, export performance and Harrod's trade multiplier', *O.E.P.*, 31: 303–23.

(1983): 'Import and export ratios and the dynamic Harrod trade multiplier: a reply to McGregor and Swales', *O.E.P.*, 35: 125–9.

Kindleberger, C.P. (1956): *The Terms of Trade: A European Case Study*, MIT, New York.

118   **References**

Krishna, K. (1983): 'Trade restrictions as facilitating practices', Manuscript, Princeton University.

Krugman, P. (1982): 'The macroeconomics of protection with a floating exchange rate', *Carnegie-Rochester Conference Series on Public Policy*, 16: 141–82, North-Holland, Amsterdam.

(1984): 'Import protection as export promotion: international competition in the presence of oligopoly and economies of scale', in H. Kierzkowski (ed.) *Monopolistic Competition in International Trade*, Oxford University Press.

(1987): 'Is free trade passe?', *Economic Perspectives*, 1: 131–44.

Laursen, S. and Metzler, L. (1950): 'Flexible exchange rates and the theory of employment', *Review of Economics and Statistics*, 32: 281–99.

Leak, H. (1937): 'Some results of the import duties act', *J.R.S.S.*, 100, Part IV: 558–95.

Lewis, W.A. (1949): *Economic Survey, 1919–1939*.

(1952): 'World production prices and trade 1870–1960', *The Manchester School*, 20: 105–38.

(1978): *Growth and Fluctuations 1870–1913*, George Allen & Unwin, London.

Liepmann, H. (1938): *Tariff Levels and the Economic Unity of Europe*, George Allen & Unwin, London.

Lomax, K.S. (1959): 'Production and productivity movements in the United Kingdom since 1900', *J.R.S.S.*, 2, Series A: 185–220.

(1969): 'Growth and productivity in the United Kingdom', in D.H. Aldcroft and P. Fearon (eds.), *Economic Growth in 20th-Century Britain*, Macmillan, London.

London and Cambridge Economic Service (various editions): *Monthly Bulletin*, London.

Maddison, A. (1967): 'Comparative Productivity Levels in the Development Countries', *Banca, Nazionale Del Lavoro Quarterly Review*, 83: 295–315.

(1979): 'Long Run Dynamics of Productivity Growth', *Banca Nazionale Del Lavoro Quarterly Review*, 128: 3–44.

(1980): 'Phases of Capital Development', in R.C.O. Matthews (ed.), *Economic Growth and Resources: Vol. 2, Trends and Factors*, London.

(1982): *Phases of Capitalist Development*, Oxford University Press.

Maizels, A. (1963): *Industrial Growth and World Trade*, Cambridge University Press.

Matthews, K.G.P. (1986): 'Was sterling overvalued in 1925?', *Ec.H.R.*, 39: 572–87.

Matthews, R.C.O., Feinstein, C.H. and Odling-Smee, J.C. (1982): *British Economic Growth, 1856–1973*, Oxford University Press.

McCloskey, D.N. (1970): 'Did Victorian Britain fail?', *Ec.H.R.*, 23: 446–59.

(1974): 'Victorian growth: a rejoinder', *Ec.H.R.*, 27: 275–7.

McCombie, J.S.L. (1985): 'Economic growth, the Harrod foreign trade multiplier and the Hicks' super multiplier', *Applied Economics*, 17: 55–72.

Metzler, L.A. (1949): 'Tariffs, the terms of trade, and the distribution of national income', *J.P.E.*, 62: 1–29.

Middleton, R. (1981): 'The constant employment budget balance and British budgetary policy, 1929–39', *Ec.H.R.*, 34: 266–86.

Mitchell, B.R. (1980): *European Historical Statistics 1750–1970*, Macmillan, London.
  (1982): *International Historical Statistics: Africa and Asia*, Macmillan, London.
  (1983): *International Historical Statistics: The Americas and Australasia*, Macmillan, London.
  (1988): *Abstract of British Historical Statistics*, Cambridge University Press.
Moggridge, D.E. (1969): *British Monetary Policy, 1924–31: The Norman Conquest of $4.86*, Cambridge University Press.
  (1981): 'Financial crises and lenders of last resort: policy in the crises of 1920 and 1929', *Journal of European Economic History*, 10: 47–69.
Morgan, A.D. and Martin, D. (1975): 'Tariff reductions and UK imports of manufactures: 1955–71', *National Institute Economics Review*, 72, May: (1952) 38–54.
Morgan, E.V. (1952): *Studies in British Financial Policy, 1914–1925*, Macmillan, London.
Mundell, R.A. (1961): 'Flexible exchange rates and employment policy', *Canadian Journal of Economics*, 27: 509–17.
Neisser, H. (1948): 'The Propensity of Industrial Countries to Import Manufactured Goods', Institute of World Affairs, New York.
Nevin, E. (1955): *The Mechanism of Cheap Money*, University of Wales, Cardiff.
Obsfeld, M. (1982): 'Aggregate spending and the terms-of-trade: is there a Laursen-Metzler effect?', *Quarterly Journal of Economics*, 97: 251–70.
OECD (1987): *Structural Adjustment and Economic Performance*, Paris.
Pigou, A.C. (1947): *Aspects of British Economic History, 1919–1925*, Frank Cass and Co. Ltd, London.
Pollard, S. (ed.), *The Gold Standard and Employment Policies between the Wars*, Methuen, London.
Pressnell, L.S. (1978): '1925: the burden of sterling', *Ec.H.R.* 31: 57–88.
Reddaway, W.B. (1970): 'Was $4.86 inevitable in 1925?', *Lloyds Bank Review*, 96: 15–28.
Redmond, J. (1980): 'An indicator of the effective exchange rate of the pound in the nineteen-thirties', *Ec.H.R.*, 33: 83–91.
  (1981): 'More effective exchange rates in the nineteen-thirties: North America and the gold bloc', Discussion Paper Series D, No. 8, Faculty of Commerce and Social Science, University of Birmingham.
  (1984): 'The sterling overvaluation in 1925: a multilateral approach', *Ec.H.R.*, 37: 520–32.
Richardson, H.W. (1967): *Economic Recovery in Britain, 1932–9*, Weidenfeld and Nicolson, London.
Robertson, A.J. (1983): 'British rearmament and industrial growth, 1935–1939', in P. Uselding (ed.), *Research in Economic History*, 8: 278–98, JAI, London.
Sayers, R.S. (1960): 'The return to gold, 1925', in L.S. Pressnell (ed.), *Studies in the Industrial Revolution*, Athlone, University of London.
Scott, M.F.G. (1963): *A Study of United Kingdom Imports*, Cambridge University Press.

Solomou, S.N. (1987): *Phases of Economic Growth, 1850–1973: Kondratieff Waves and Kuznets Swings*, Cambridge University Press.

Solomou, S.N. and Weale, M.R. (1988): 'British Economic Growth, 1870–1913: Facts and Artefacts', Department of Applied Economics Working Paper No. 886.

Svennilson, I. (1952): *Growth and Stagnation in the European Economy*, U.N.E.C.E., Geneva.

Svensson, L.E.O. and Razin, A. (1983): 'The terms-of-trade and the current account: the Harberger-Laursen-Metzler effect', *J.P.E.*, 91: 97–125.

Thirlwall, A.P. (1979): 'The balance of payments constraint as an explanation of international growth rate differences', *Banca Nazionale Del Lavoro Quarterly Review*, 128: 44–53.

(1982): 'The Harrod trade multiplier and the importance of export-led growth', *Pakistan Journal of Applied Economics*, 1: 1–21.

Thomas, M. (1983): 'Rearmament and economic recovery in the late 1930s', *Ec.H.R.*, 36: 559–79.

Thomas, T.J. (1976): 'Aspects of UK macroeconomic policy during the interwar period: a study in econometric history', Ph.D. Thesis, Cambridge.

(1981): 'Aggregate demand in the United Kingdom 1918–45', in R. Floud and D.N. McCloskey (eds.), *The Economic History of Britain Since 1700* Vol. 2, Cambridge University Press.

Tower, E. (1973): 'Commercial policy under fixed and flexible exchange rates', *Quarterly Journal of Economics*, 87: 436–54.

Venables, A.J. and Smith, A. (1986): 'Trade and industrial policy under imperfect competition', *Economic Policy*, 1: 622–72.

Von Tunzelmann, G.N. (1982): 'Structural change and leading sectors in British manufacturing 1907–68', in C.P. Kindleberger and G. di Tella (eds.), *Economics in the Long View*, Vol. III, Macmillan, London.

Worswick, G.D.N. (1984): 'Economic recovery in the 1930s', *National Institute Economic Review*, 110: 85–93.

Wright, J.F. (1981): 'Britain's interwar experience', in W.A. Eltis and P.J.N. Sinclair (eds.), *The Money Supply and Exchange Rate*, Oxford University Press.

Youngson, A.J. (1960): *The British Economy 1920–1957*, George Allen & Unwin, London.

Index of names

Barna, T. 35
Beenstock, M. 7, 16, 20, 43, 96
Birkett 37
Boyer, R. 26
Brander, J.A. 25, 102
Broadberry, S.N. 39, 89–90

Capie, F. 2, 3, 22, 33, 36–9, 56, 83, 96
Chan, K. 27
Corden, W.M. 25
Crafts, N.F.R. 1, 9

Dimsdale, N.H. 16, 96–8
Dixit, A.K. 25
Dowie, J.A. 10, 14

Eichengreen, B. 1, 12, 27, 39, 40, 90

Fienstein, C.H. 9, 10, 11, 13, 17
Ford, J.L. 26, 27
Foreman–Peck, J. 38–9

Grassman, S. 19, 48
Greasley, D. 8

Harrod, H. 28
Hatton, T.J. 1, 12
Houthakker, H.S. 51

Kaldor, N. 18, 28–9
Keynes, J.M. 2
Krugman, P. 25, 27, 102

Laursen, S. 26, 27
Leak, H. 1–3, 50, 66
Lewis, W.A. 5, 12, 68
Lomax, K.S. 12, 14, 15, 16

Magee, S.D. 51
Maddison, A. 7, 13
Martin, D. 52
Matthews, R.C.O. 8, 10, 43
Metzler, L.A. 26, 27
Middleton, R. 92–3
Morgan, A.D. 52
Mundell, R.A. 26, 27

Redmond, J. 89, 90
Richardson, H. 22, 34–6, 73–4, 83, 90, 92

Sachs, J. 90
Sen, S. 26, 27
Smith. A. 102
Solomou, S.N. 8, 9, 10, 13
Stone, R. 9

Tunzelmann, G.N. von 98

Warburton, P. 96
Warwick, G.D.N. 92
Weale, M. 8, 10

Venables, A.J. 102

Subject index

Printed in the United States
72477LV00002B/13